THE NEW YORK VISION

Interpretations of
New York City
in the
American Novel

ROBERT A. GATES

UNIVERSITY
PRESS OF
AMERICA

Copyright © 1987 by
University Press of America,® Inc.

4720 Boston Way
Lanham, MD 20706

Printed in the United States of America

Library of Congress Cataloging-in-Publication Data

Gates, Robert Allan.
  The New York vision.

  Bibliography: p.
  Includes index.
  1. American fiction—History and criticism.
2. New York (N.Y.) in literature. 3. Cities and towns
in literature. 4. American fiction—New York (N.Y.)—
History and criticism. I. Title.
PS374.N43G38   1987   813'.009'327471   87-5054
ISBN 0-8191-6270-1 (pbk. : alk. paper)
ISBN 0-8191-6269-8 (hard : alk. paper)

All University Press of America books are produced on acid-free
paper which exceeds the minimum standards set by the National
Historical Publication and Records Commission.

FOR KATHY

ACKNOWLEDGMENTS

I wish to thank the publishers of the following authors for permission to reprint extracts from their works:

Saul Bellow—from *Mr. Sammler's Planet*, copyright © 1969, 1970 by Saul Bellow. Reprinted by permission of Viking-Penguin Inc.

John Cheever—from *Bullet Park*, copyright © 1967, 1968, 1969 by John Cheever. Reprinted by permission of Alfred A. Knopf, Inc.

John Dos Passos—from *Manhattan Transfer*, copyright © 1925, 1953 by John Dos Passos. Reprinted by permission of Elizabeth H. Dos Passos, co-executor, estate of John Dos Passos.

Nathanael West—from *Miss Lonelyhearts and The Day of the Locust*, copyright © 1933 by Nathanael West; renewed © 1939 by the Estate of Nathanael West; renewed © 1960 by Laura Perelman (*Miss Lonelyhearts*); renewed © 1966 by Laura Perelman.

Thomas Wolfe—from *Of Time and the River*, copyright © 1935 by Charles Scribner's Sons; renewed © 1963 by Paul Gitlin, Administrator, C.T.A. Reprinted by permission of Charles Scribner's Sons.

TABLE OF CONTENTS

INTRODUCTION

Those who choose to write about New York City face a substantial challenge since their City is by far the most dynamic, varied, and perplexing in the world. There are no standards the novelist can grasp; no guidelines he can follow; methods incorporated by other writers are inadequate for him. The City presents no standard language, philosophy, or neighborhood that can be labelled as typically New York. If the writer pursues his objective despite these obstacles, he will most likely be unappreciated by a reading public, critics, and publishers who have their own cherished perceptions of the City.

The purpose of our study is to examine how novelists from different times and governed by different circumstances have overcome these obstacles in their works about New York. Each chapter is divided in focus. The first part examines the historical City, how it existed, and its evolution during a particular time. The remainder is devoted to an analysis of major literary works produced during that period. By doing this, a comparison between the "actual" City and the "fictional" City can be drawn as well as a comparison between the reality surrounding the novelist and his perception of that reality.

The reality, itself, was a long time in the making. New York's history extended back into the seventeenth century, but its identity, its personality as a city, would not be clearly defined until the nineteenth century. Throughout the eighteenth century New York remained a provincial town—not unlike Philadelphia or Boston—that derived its identity in comparison with European cities. It was described as another Liverpool, a developing London, a rival of Paris—but it never existed on its own terms.

Two events at the beginning of the nineteenth century changed all this. One was the War of 1812 which definitively altered America's self-opinion. When peace was signed, America considered itself not only politically independent but psychologically free from the influence of England and Europe. This in turn altered New York's self-image and helped untie her provincial apron strings with British cities. Furthermore, the completion of the Erie Canal during the 1820's established New York as the dominant mercantile center of the United States, far outstripping her former rivals, Boston and Philadelphia. By the time of the Civil War, New York's identity as America's dominant center of trade and culture was firmly established. But her growth had been so rapid and haphazard that many questioned her new status and its effect on her inhabitants.

Two authors that explore the City during these early, turbulent years are James Fenimore Cooper and Herman Melville. In *Home as Found*, Cooper reflects upon a physical city that is fast abandoning its early Colonial customs and appearance for a pseudo-European elegance. The process has left everyone confused and especially one family, the Effingham's, who have recently returned from a lengthy stay abroad. In Melville's *Bartleby*, however, it is not the developing City that is perplexing but rather the moral ambivalence created by that development. The physical City in *Bartleby* is completed. The stone and brick facades of the modern city have already taken shape and are now exerting a subtle influence on the City's inhabitants, affecting their humanity or lack of it and their purpose in life.

The confusion manifest in the novels of Cooper and Melville is again found in works on the City appearing at the end of the nineteenth century, but with a difference. By this time another significant change had occurred in the character of New York City. Post-Civil War prosperity and the opening of the West had encouraged massive waves of immigrants to seek success in the new world, and the first port-of-call for most was New York. Many stayed and established large ethnic neighborhoods. Some succeeded, but many likewise failed, and New York saw for the first time in its history the rise of tenement slums. Poverty had now become a major aspect of the developing City, contrasting sharply with the mansions of the industrialists and bankers of upper Fifth Avenue. The City was polarized with clearly defined borders between the lifestyles and habitations of the rich and the poor. Nor was there a large middle class to act as a buffer between the two extremes. It had begun to form within the ghettoes with the rise of successful merchants and tradesmen, and would not exert a considerable influence on the City until well into the twentieth century.

Two novelists who capture these times in their novels are Edith Wharton and Stephen Crane. Each, however, tends to focus on that part of the City he or she knows best. For Wharton, it is the world of the rich. Born into an affluent New York family, she could easily write about the lifestyles of her rich neighbors and friends. She was familiar with their virtues and their failings as well as the self-imposed limitations placed upon them by their environment. To the outsider they presented an air of grandeur that seemed to rise above the ordinary preoccupations and hassles of everyday people. But Wharton knew better. She realized that it was a lifestyle masking a hollowness of soul, a degenerate selfishness doomed to eventual extinction. And this is the truth her heroine, Lily Bart, realizes in the closing pages of *The House of Mirth*.

This was not Crane's world. As a newspaper reporter and adherent to the developing trend toward literary realism, Crane found his inspiration in the slums of New York. Here was a world about which little, if anything, had been written. It was a world whose brutal dimensions could not be compromised in print. It demanded reality, and Crane presents it with candor in his novelette, *Maggie: A Girl of the Streets*. Ironically, his conclusions are not too different from those of Wharton, for Crane's world is one that also relies heavily on masks and is inherently self-destructive at its core. Also, both novelists conclude with an apocalyptic vision of the City—a polarized city perched on the brink of destruction.

But contrary to their predictions, the City did not die but was saved in a manner that neither could foresee—saved by its own mutability, its ability to rapidly change with the times. In each decade following World War One, New York evolved faster than it had throughout the entire last half of the nineteenth century. During the 1920's, it exhibited this dynamism on three levels— economic, intellectual, and social. Wall Street became the symbol of America's post-War prosperity, and the rumors of massive fortunes being made by ordinary people every day were not untrue. The optimism of a nation that could not or would not conceive of anyone remaining poor if only he "played the market" permeated every corner of the business world of lower Manhattan and stimulated an atmosphere of liberal thought.

Examples of such thought appeared on both the intellectual and social levels. New York led the cultural movement in America, and its Greenwich Village neighborhood reflected all that was distinctively avant garde, progressive, and artistic. It became the birthplace of countless artistic magazines, art galleries, and Bohemian hang-outs. One boarding house off Washington Square that sheltered such luminaries as Theodore Dreiser, Stephen Crane, Frank Norris, Willa Cather, and Eugene O'Neill was rightfully dubbed the "House of Genius." Within this world, the literary and artistic traditions of the past were rapidly abandoned and replaced with the new and the innovative. New Yorkers in general also broke free from the social traditions of their ancestors. Women bobbed their hair; hemlines rose; socialist ideas were espoused; children rebelled against their parents; and a growing atmosphere of lawlessness that openly flaunted the restrictions of Prohibition swept the City.

One writer possessed by these times was John Dos Passos, and no writer, before or since, captures more successfully the City in all its confusing variety. Finding the formats of conventional novels inappropriate, Dos Passos creates a kaleidoscopic effect in *Manhattan Transfer* by developing multiple viewpoints that continually merge and separate with the passing of time. Here at last is novel that breaks from the traditional practice of using New York as a backdrop for the action. Instead, the City becomes the principal character in the action, a living entity.

However, by the 1930's the Great Depression signalled a new era for the City. Gone was the ebullience of the 1920's and its carefree abandonment of tradition. The 1930's were a time of retrospection and soul-searching, a time of doubt and despair. As in the 1920's, the City again became a symbol of the decade. The Depression had begun there with the Wall Street panic on Black Tuesday, October 1929, and every image of despair, every bread line, every homeless person in heartland America could be seen on its streets.

One writer about the City at this time was a visitor from the South—Thomas Wolfe. His mammoth novel, *Of Time and the River*, devotes its "Proteus" section, almost a novel in itself, to the Depression City. The perspective presented through the eyes of its principal character, Eugene Gant, is grim. Walking the streets between his hotel room and his teaching job at the university, Gant is at first upset and then obsessed with the brutality, ugliness, and cold-heartedness surrounding him. The City belies his original perception of it as being enchanted and dreamlike, and instead becomes a prison for his soul, harboring all that is destructive to man's better instincts—a city of despair—morally as well as economically.

Another novelist, Nathanael West, uses a different approach. For him, the City offers a surrealistic landscape of brutality and false dreams. His novelette, *Miss Lonelyhearts*, is not presented within the realistic framework of a narrator's perception, but rather a crazy-quilt interaction of bizarre, irrational, and degenerate characters. The plot is immaterial when the disease is so overwhelming, and New York is a diseased City inhabited by a diseased humanity infected with the disease of the Great Depression.

The optimism of the 1920's and the despair of the 1930's have appeared intermittently and equally in the consciousness of New York City since World War Two. The ambivalence that has ensued has become the trademark of the contemporary City. In the years immediately following the War, New York retained its cultural and economic superiority but lost ground as an attractive place in which to live. Thousands of returning veterans who had grown up on the avenues of Brooklyn or the Bronx sought out the tree-lined streets of suburbia for their families. For them and many others, the City was no place for raising children; the air was polluted; the streets dangerous; recreational facilities were woefully inadequate. Suburbia offered a superior lifestyle, better schools, and freedom from, it seemed, all the ills that plagued the urban dweller.

But suburbia had another side, a side that became increasingly evident with the passing of time. As the population skyrocketed, existing public services were strained far beyond their capabilities. Schools became inadequate, mass transit unreliable, roads impassable, and the overall quality of life began to decline. Most disturbing was the increase in crime, especially violent crime. Assaults, rapes, and even murders appeared with increasing regularity. The assault on the bastion of tranquility was complete, as many suburbanites vainly triple locked their doors against the inevitable. No place in America seemed safe anymore.

Such changeable and highly confusing times inevitably result in the explosion of myths. The City cannot be definitively classified as either declining or improving. The direction of its future depends upon one's point of view. And the same can be said about suburbia as well. Two writers who express this viewpoint are Saul Bellow and John Cheever. Their orientations are different, however. Bellow is concerned with the City and examines it through the eyes of an aging Polish Jew, Mr. Artur Sammler, in *Mr. Sammler's Planet*. Cheever's protagonist is Mr. Eliot Nailles, an inhabitant of the seemingly tranquil and dangerously naive suburban world of *Bullet Park*.

For Mr. Sammler, an intellectual with the manners and customs of a genteel pre-War Europe, the City is a modern enigma as well as a reflection of his own past. He is at odds with its assault on the senses and disgraceful lack of manners but finds in its violence, its mindless anarchy, parallels to the destruction of civilization he witnessed during the War in Nazi-dominated Europe. On its streets is staged the future of humanity and all its varied races, either coexisting in relative harmony or doomed to extinction. New York City, for Sammler, is the universal city of man and a harbinger of things to come.

On the surface, the world of Eliot Nailles seems vastly different—tranquil and idyllic. But this is a myth, for underneath the suburban setting lurks all the ills of mankind. Nailles, along with his neighbors, has made a common suburban mistake; he believes that a change in environment automatically effects a change in the way people behave and act toward one another. But when his son lapses into progressive imbecility and a neighbor commits suicide, Nailles can only find solace in drugs, the ultimate withdrawal from pain in a suburban world that offers no tangible method of dealing with grief. Thus, for both novelists, the future is as uncertain as the modern dimensions of the City which has now expanded beyond its physical boundary and encompasses a new consciousness—nebulous, uncertain, and still developing.

Robert A. Gates
St. John's University

THE NEW YORK VISION:

Interpretations of New York City in the American Novel

CHAPTER I

The Developing City:
James Fenimore Cooper's
Home As Found
and Herman Melville's *Bartleby*

New York City during the first half of the nineteenth century was a city in search of itself. It was a city that was rapidly discarding its pre-Revolutionary War provincialism for a confusing and sometimes unnerving atmosphere of change and development. Nothing seemed to be constant. Its business environment changed so rapidly and grew so alarmingly that it fueled an atmosphere of unlicensed speculation unchecked except for the occasional, devastating depressions that appeared from time to time. The City's population similarly grew and changed as emigrants from Ireland and Germany dominated large areas of the City, influencing its social customs, religious orientation, cultural pursuits, and politics. Concomitant to the sudden rise in population were the growing incidents of crime and violence almost unheard of during the early provincial years. The City's efforts to adjust to these and other problems of growth were evidenced in its increasing city services. Police and fire protection had to be expanded. Inner-city transportation had to be improved. And they were, but at the cost of an increasing bureaucracy that was frequently condemned for internal corruption and racketeering. In short, nothing less than the entire culture of the City was evolving. But the benefits were debatable. Old New Yorkers frequently mourned the demolition of buildings and even entire neighborhoods that they had known as youngsters. The City's mood was in step with its youth. But youth is temperamental and quixotic, and the average New Yorker found

3

himself at a psychological crossroads—trying to remember a disappearing past and unable to fathom the future. For the New Yorker of the early nineteenth century, nothing seemed constant.

From its early Dutch days, New York had been preeminently a commercial city. This was to be expected since Manhattan Island was unfit for extensive agricultural development. Its excellent harbor at the base of the Hudson River Valley made it uniquely suited for trade. Farmland was to be found to the East in Brooklyn or to the West in New Jersey, but for Manhattan only counting houses and stores could grow rapidly on its rocky and unfertile soil. During the eighteenth century the City's growth was slow. This was due in part to its competition with the ports of Philadelphia and Boston, both of which frequently claimed economic superiority to New York harbor. A post-War New York, however, rapidly outstripped these rivals, the reason for this being a complex and interrelated series of events.

The most decisive factor in the City's post-War economic growth was inevitably the Erie Canal. Completed in 1825, its effect was immediate and dramatic. Within the first year nearly five hundred new merchants opened shops in the City, as did twelve new banks and thirteen new marine insurance firms. The impact, in fact, was so great it prompted one German visitor to the City to speculate that practically the "whole commerce of the country" was passing through the port of New York, a viewpoint not entirely exaggerated since the new City captured over one-half of the Nation's imports and nearly one-third of its exports.[1] What made the Canal so eminently successful was its ability to open the Middle West via a complex set of waterways stretching from Lake Erie to Albany, and from there via the Hudson River to New York. It became, as one critic has aptly noted, the "Nation's golden cord."[2]

Alongside the Canal, other forms of transportation were soon expanded, further enhancing the City's potential as a major trade center. By 1851, the completion of the Erie and Hudson River railroads established further links with the West and an even more extensive Western market. The Cunard Line had also recently moved its terminal from Boston to New York, thereby giving the City an additional advantage in both domestic and foreign commerce.

As New York became increasingly a center for transporting goods from Europe to the Middle West, a rage for land speculation began. As early as the 1830's, many were confident that former farmland or residential properties would soon be needed for the new business that would handle the growing trade. One foreign visitor noted in 1835 that "Everybody is speculating, and everything has become an object of speculation."[3] An eminent New York businessman, Philip Hone, observed in his diary of the same year how "Men in moderate circumstances have become immensely rich merely by the good fortune of owning farms of a few acres of chosen land."[4] As land rapidly exchanged hands from day to day and prices spiraled rapidly upward, the City's psychological self-image was transformed from what had once been a relatively calm pre-War provincialism to a bustling "go-getting" atmosphere that, along with the practical advantages created by the Erie Canal and the railroads, stimulated an unprecedented growth within the business community. Hone summed up the new atmosphere when he wrote in his diary for 1835 about the "prosperous state" in the country as a whole and New York in particular:

> All descriptions of property are higher than I have ever known them. Money is plenty, business brisk, the staple commodity of the country (cotton) has enriched all through whose hands it has passed, the merchant, mechanic, and proprietor of land all rejoice in the result of the last year's operations. As for myself, I have availed myself of the rise of property, and sold enough to clear me of debt, which has been my great object for a year past. . . . I have gotten myself comparatively easy and comfortable, enjoying my armchair and the luxuries of my library.[5]

The prosperity that Hone and his contemporaries encountered encouraged an ever-increasing prosperity since the new affluent New Yorker preferred the costly products of Europe to less expensive domestic articles. Europe, and especially England, were only too eager to satisfy this demand. Inventories in Europe had increased enormously during the War of 1812 when trade was brought almost to a standstill. Now, with the peace and the following "era of good relations," foreign manufacturers dumped most of their surpluses in America through the port of New York. Great fleets were launched even before orders were received. The prosperity that ensued from this increasing trade firmly established New York's preeminence as the business center of America. It was a preeminence that would remain uninterrupted into the twentieth century—uninterrupted by depressions and wars.

As New York's reputation grew as a city of ever-expanding trade and commerce, it captured more than the attention of European merchants and manufacturers; it also became the dream city for thousands of immigrants who considered it a golden chance for economic opportunity. Between 1815 and 1860 the City grew from less than 100,000 to over 800,000. Nearly 70% of all aliens entering America entered through the Port of New York, and many stayed on to establish businesses, schools, theatres and affect practically every aspect of city life. New Yorkers and foreign visitors commented alike on the growing cosmopolitan ambiance of the City free, finally, as one noted, from the "air of a provincial town."[6] By the 1860's the outline of the modern twentieth-century city could already be seen. New York had certainly one of the most varied populations in the world and certainly the most varied in the United States.

But the City's population was growing faster and the City's border expanding quicker than anyone had predicted. There was no adequate water supply. The existing one was antiquated, relied on wooden pipes that frequently broke and wells that often ran dry. At times river water had to be substituted for well water, and the drinking water became decidedly brakish and polluted. The wealthy used bottled water, but for many inhabitants the only source of water was the municipal pump down the street; and no matter how polluted it was, it was all that was available. Understandably, the City was beseiged by numerous cholera epidemics and dysentery frequently took a sizeable toll during the summer months. Common sewers were practically non-existent. All garbage was left out on the street where it was supposed to be carted and dumped into the rivers on both sides of Manhattan. But here too city services were often unreliable, and the garbage frequently became the sport of scavenger pigs used by the City as garbage disposals as late as the 1840's. "The streets of New York are not to be perambulated with impunity by either the lame, or the blind, or the exquisitely sensitive in their olfactory nerves," a Glasgow visitor wisely observed.[7] Further compounding the hazards of an urban stroller were the broken pavements, frequent absence of sidewalks, and poor lighting. These, along with inadequate police protection, made a leisurely walk along the byways of New York positively dangerous.

Visitors to the City frequently questioned why such industrious people as New Yorkers failed to improve their services to an adequate level. What they failed to realize was that these services were being improved continually, but failed to keep pace with the rapidly expanding City. Long-range planning was practically impossible until 1860. One visitor, Henry Philip Tappan, Chancellor of the University of Michigan, prophetically observed that "all the works of the present busy and prosperous generation sink into insignificance," with each passing day. "The New York of to-day," he continued, "is not the New York of fifty years ago; and fifty years hence where will the New York of to-day be?"[8]

Further compounding the problem, as many saw it, was rampant political corruption. George Templeton Strong underlined this as the major factor in all the City's woes and fumed in his diary that "to be a citizen of New York is a disgrace. . . . The New Yorker belongs to a community worse governed by lower and baser blackguard scum than any city in Western Christendom."[9] Strong's lament was well-founded for around him he saw such notorious gangsters as Isaiah Rynders, the undisputed ruler of the Five Points, rise to the position of United States Marshal, while his crony, Fernando Wood, became the boss of Tammany Hall and was twice elected Mayor. But all was not bleak and grim in early New York. Many civic-minded citizens like Hone and Strong banded together to push through reforms. Without these reforms, as they and others justly noted, the City's effective expansion would eventually be hurt and business would suffer. Certain reforms were therefore necessary in order to secure the City's preeminence.

One reform that everyone applauded was the opening of the Croton waterworks in 1842. An engineering marvel, it fascinated most New Yorkers like Hone and Strong, who made extensive comments of it in their diaries when the first water appeared from the Croton River forty miles away. Strong happily noted in his diary entry for June 28th that finally "Croton Water is slowly flowing toward the City, which at last will stand a chance of being cleaned—if water *can* clean it."[10] Strong and his friends, however, were somewhat reserved about drinking the first amount of water to issue from the pipes out of fear that during the construction of the waterway every worker had inevitably used it "as a necessity." "I shall drink no Croton for some time to come." He cautiously concluded, "Jekial Post has drunk some of it and is in dreadful apprehension of breeding bullfrogs inwardly."[11] European visitors

who were familiar with the City's past water problems were more
ecstatic. Sir Charles Tyell, a Scottish geologist, rapsodized that the
project was,

> more akin in magnificence to the ancient and modern Roman aque-
> ducts . . . The health of the city is said to have already gained by
> greater cleanliness and more wholesome water for drinking. . . .
> The water can be carried to the attics of every house, and many are
> introducing baths and indulging in ornamental fountains in private
> gardens. The rate of insurance for fire has been lowered; and I could
> not help reflecting as I looked at the moving water, at a season when
> every pond is covered with ice, how much more security the city
> must now enjoy than during the great conflagration in the winter of
> 1835 when there was such a want of water to supply the
> engines. . . .[12]

In a similar tone, Hone praised the "wholesome temperance bev-
erage, well calculated to cool the palates and quench the thirst of
the New Yorker, and to diminish the losses of the fire insurance
companies."[13]

The sudden expansion of business, immigration, and city services also began to shape the cultural image of New York and its
inhabitants by the mid-nineteenth century. Throughout the eighteenth century the City remained undefined except in comparison
with the great European cities of London and Paris. But by the
mid-1800's the City had tentatively established a distinct self-
image—a clearly defined concept of what New York was and what
it was to be a New Yorker. The tumultuousness of the business
scene was the primary influence on this cultural self-image. It repeatedly dictated a standard of living for all New Yorkers—rich and
poor alike. On one level it helped spur the "democratic ferment"
of the City, frequently noted by visitors who commented on the
surprising well-being of the working people and the democratic
attitudes of all New Yorkers in general. Nor could a permanent,
monied class develop since speculation in real estate and the stock
market both made and unmade investors every day. "Fortunes are
made and lost by a single speculation," one observer noted. "There
is comparatively no settled and permanent body of leading capitalists, and consequently far less room for that sort of defensive
league which naturally takes place among men of common interests and position in society."[14] Business further established the
"tone" of the City in that all activities were carried out in the

fastest manner imaginable. Nothing, one visitor observed, "nothing in the world could stop or divert the torrent. Even if Sebastopol had been in their way, those men would have run over it at one rush."[15] And, finally, other visitors commented on how the business environment nurtured new values. "New Yorkers seem to live to make money and spend it" was the concluding observation of two English visitors in the City during the 1840's.[16]

By the mid-1800's this "business tempo" extended to all aspects of city life. It shaped the architecture of the City where few buildings remained permanent very long. Conservative New Yorkers were appalled to find most of the landmarks of their youth disappearing before their eyes. Hone frequently found streets blocked because of new construction or the demolition of "old" buildings. "Pearl Street and Broadway," he lamented, "are rendered almost impassable by the quantity of rubbish with which they are obstructed, and by the dust which is blown about by a keen northwest wind."[17] In 1856, *Harpers Magazine* complained that a "man born in New York forty years ago finds nothing, absolutely nothing, of the New York he knew. If he chances to stumble upon a few old houses not yet leveled, he is fortunate."[18]

Similarly, Hone and his friends decried the lack of any distinctive architecture in New York where there was "scarcely a public building deserving of notice."[19] The English actress, Frances Kemble, was nonplussed by the "irregular collection of temporary buildings" that the city landscape presented.[20] These and other commentators on New York hoped that eventually a distinctively American architecture would appear as the City became more mature. But what they failed to realize was that the distinctiveness of the New York scene lay in its non-distinctiveness. The stage was already set for the future City where a business environment would forever preclude the establishment of any permanent architecture, and where change would become representative of the City's character.

Only two aspects of the City's architecture seemed to remain relatively constant and increase with each passing year—the ever-increasing vertical growth of Manhattan's buildings, "high growths of iron, slender, strong . . . splendidly uprising toward clear skies,"[21] as Walt Whitman would note in the 1850's, and, second, the growing predominance of glass in urban structures. One of the first buildings to exhibit a profuse, and, according to Hone, dangerously unwarranted amount of glass was the A.T. Stewart department store completed in 1846. It was fronted by huge plate glass windows which, Hone warned, would most likely become the target of a rock. "I am greatly mistaken," Hone vowed, "if there are not persons (one is enough) in this heterogeneous mass of population influenced by jealousy, malice, or other instigation of the devil, bad enough to do such a deed of mischief."[22]

The City's fast business pace dominated more than architectural development, however. It set the pace for gustatory attractions as well from the homely "Oyster Saloons" to the fashionable restaurants catering to the *beau monde*. Everything was expected to be ordered, consumed and paid for with the utmost haste. Entertainment, too, was carried out in a fast manner. So fast, indeed, that in 1867 Mark Twain spoofed the general tone of the town when he noted:

> There is something in this ceaseless buzz, and hurry, and bustle, that keeps a stranger in a state of unwholesome excitement all the time, and makes him restless and uneasy . . . a something which impels him to try to do everything, and yet permits him to do nothing . . . A stranger feels unsatisfied, here, a good part of the time. He starts to a library; changes, and moves toward a theatre; changes again and thinks he will visit a friend; goes within a biscuit-toss of a picture-gallery, a billiard-room, a beer-cellar and a circus, in succession, and finally drifts home and to bed, without having really done anything or gone anywhere.[23]

The haphazardness of city life was further compounded by the annual ritual of landlords renewing their leases on May 31st. Neighborhoods continually changed as rents were increased. An amused English visitor to the City found the perpetual moves of New Yorkers an "intolerable nuisance,"

> but the New Yorker, no doubt from habit, not only looks upon it as a matter of course, but seems to feel an elevation of spirits at the anticipation of this agreeable variety in his social existence; and it is no uncommon circumstance to meet with individuals who have resided in a dozen different houses in as many years; and yet who speak of their wish to try the advantages of another quarter of the city when the proper season arrives.[24]

Nevertheless, cultural pockets began to form. Nowhere was this more evident than in the Bowery, where one could touch shoulders with and hear the various dialects of Irishmen, Germans, Italians, Slovak Jews, Frenchmen, Spaniards, and Orientals. To a certain extent the Bowery was self-contained and self-sufficient during the early 1800's. Its manners and customs were uniquely its own. It had its own theatres, and its turbulent night life separated it from much of the City. Within its boundaries could be found the traits of the mature City with its multifarious and complex cultural background. As the century progressed the Bowery grew to become not atypical of the City but rather a microcosm of its essence.

In time, numerous theatres were constructed, each catering to a specific type of audience. By the beginning of the Civil War, close to twenty theatres were offering a wide choice of entertainment from opera to burlesque and pulling in receipts of close to $3,000,000 in a good year. The cosmopolitan City welcomed the plays and performers from various lands, and it was not uncommon to find at any time theatrical fare featuring English, French, German, Italian, Spanish, Japanese, or Chinese productions. New York had become the theatrical center of the Nation, a preeminence impossible without its largely immigrant population.

Foreign influence found its way into other city entertainments as well. Lectures were frequently given on a variety of topics, and often foreign speakers were featured. Art shows on the developing trends among American and European artists were also all the rage. Finally, there were the fashionable balls that too reflected the growing cosmopolitan nature of the town. Practically every conceivable style of dress—American or European—could be found at the balls. The Grand Ball at the Academy of Music, given for the Prince of Wales during his American tour of 1860, put on display the City's amazing array of fashion and helped establish New York as a fashion center, second only to Paris. Visitors to the City were astonished at how its earlier provincial atmosphere had given way to a sophistication where even the townhouses were "gorgeously fitted up with satin and velvet draperies, rich Axminster carpets, marble and inlaid tables, and large looking-glasses. . . ."[25] The modern City had, at last, taken dimension, a point Walt Whitman would summarize in *Democratic Vistas* in 1870:

> The assemblages of the citizens in their groups, conversations, trades, evening amusements . . . these, I say, and the like of these, completely satisfy my senses of power, fulness, motion, &c., and give me, through such senses . . . a continued exaltation and absolute fulfilment. Always and more and more . . . I realize . . . that not Nature alone is great in her fields of freedom and the open air, in her storms, the shows of night and day, the mountains, forests,

11

seas—but in the artificial, the work of man too is equally great—in this profusion of teeming humanity—in these ingenuities, streets, goods, houses, ships—these hurrying, feverish, electric crowds of men, their complicated business genius, (not least among the geniuses,) and all this might, many-threaded wealth and industry concentrated here.[26]

One of the earliest accounts of New York City to be found in an American novel occurs at the beginning of James Fenimore Cooper's 1838 work, *Home as Found*. While it is unlikely that few modern critics will applaud its literary merit, it is significant, along with its companion novel, *Homeward Bound*, published in the same year, as marking Cooper's return to novel writing after a hiatus of four years since 1834 when he "retired" as a novelist in *A Letter to His Countrymen* and settled down on his estate in Cooperstown.[27]

As literary works, both novels have never been considered by Cooper scholars as ranking among the author's better productions. The prose is awkward, the situations confused and often trite, and the characters rarely rise above being mere caricatures of personalities and opinions that Cooper wants to project. Cooper's presence is naggingly persistent from one passage to the next. And, yet, if viewed in the context of the times in which they were written, the novels offer fascinating accounts of the American scene of manners and opinions in general and New York City in particular.

Paging through *Home As Found*, the reader benefits from the realization that the novel was conceived not as a separate work but rather as a sequel to *Homeward Bound*, and that both works were primarily intended as a presentation of Cooper's views in response to protracted libel suits and personal attacks brought against him by politically inspired peers. The motives behind the charges and counter-charges do not bear repetition. But as one critic has aptly noted, the events led Cooper to significantly alter his thematic orientation. While in his previous works he had warned Americans about European influences on their culture and development as a people, he now attempts to warn them about themselves.[28]

In *Home As Found*, Cooper presents his case by creating caricatures that represent specific American or European points of view. His basic message is that while America is still dangerously subservient to Europe (an opinion expressed in his earlier works), it has also grown paradoxically uncompromising and arrogant regarding its own virtues. This premise is repeatedly stated through the reactions of the Effingham family that has returned to America after an extended stay in Europe.

During the first third of *Home As Found*, Cooper creates a host of "American types" against the backdrop of New York City. Initially it seems as though the City exerts little, if any, influence on the characters presented. Indeed, much of their opinions and behavior is again found among the citizens of the upstate country town of Templeton where the majority of the novel's action takes place. Part of this is due to Cooper's deliberate intention to focus on the ideas rather than the customs of his fellow Americans. His primary goal, he notes in his preface, is to expose the "governing social evil of America . . . provincialism. . . . Every man, as a matter of course, refers to his own particular experience, and praises or condemns agreeably to notions contracted in the circle of his own habits, however narrow, provincial, or erroneous they may happen to be."[29] This, in turn, Cooper believes has created a "respectable mediocrity" in American thinking that is present everywhere—in town, city, and country alike.

But New York City's seeming failure to exercise more control over its inhabitants is also due in part to its own lack of cultural development, in contrast to European cities, and the confusion of its citizens, all of European backgrounds, who find themselves struggling with a whole new concept of living and government a mere fifty years after the Revolution. As a result, Cooper's detractors criticized the novel for having a cavalier attitude toward American "architecture, our literary institutions, our scientific associations, our political anniversaries, our foreign ambassadors, our laws, our liberties, and our modes of life."[30] Given this criticism, one could easily conclude that the novel offers a clearly detailed portrait of New York City life during the early part of the nineteenth century. But the obverse is true, with little of the physical and even social City present in the novel. Instead we find a city of ideas with each idea expressed by a particular character type.

It is from these ideas and their representative characters that a portrait of the City can be drawn. The novel presents a broad spectrum of city "types"—social climbers and the well-bred, young liberals and conservative older folks, businessmen, country lawyers, gossips and newspapermen. It is from these people and their opinions that Cooper creates his city—alive yet vague and nebulous, a developing city.

There is no doubt that the Effingham family (Edward and John, who are cousins, and Edward's daughter Eve) expresses opinions that mirror the principles and beliefs of Cooper himself. Educated and well-travelled, they represent Cooper's ideal American who can best judge his native land and fathom its weaknesses. Yet John, Edward, and Eve differ in temperament; Edward and Eve tend to be more romantically attached to their homeland, more sympathetic of its faults and quick to defend its virtues. John is more cynical, more realistic in his observation and, as such, probably more reflective of Cooper's philosophy.

The Effingham's are well-established New Yorkers with firm roots in the past and a townhouse in a fashionable section of the City. Financially independent, they have none of the insecurities of their *noveau riche* neighbors and present an example of what a New Yorker can be. They have a French governess, Mademoiselle Viefuille, whose repeated French expressions never let the reader forget her presence. But her employ is attributable more to her professional excellence than to her being French.

The Effingham family, as might be expected, find much in their town that is objectionable. Eve is disgusted by the "flirting, giggling, and childishness" of her peer group and amused that such people have pretensions of being the representatives of high society. For her, "high society" cannot exist in a city where there is little else than "balls, the morning visits, and an occasional evening in which there is no dancing." (p. 7) She recalls her visits to homes in Paris, Florence, and Rome where the hosts and guests were far more casual in their elegance and not ostentatious in their knowledge or position or childish in their behavior: "All this matter-of-course variety adds to the ease and grace of the company," she informs a friend, "and coupled with perfect good manners, a certain knowledge of passing events, pretty modes of expression, an accurate and even utterance, the women usually find the means of making themselves agreeable." (p. 8) In Chapter Eight when she leaves the City with her father to go to their country estate, she boards the steamer "to escape from a town that . . . contains so much more that is unfit for any place, in order to breathe the pure air, and enjoy the tranquil pleasure of the country." (p. 111)

Eve's sentiments are similar to her elders, John and Edward, who are appalled by the flagrant economic speculation that dominates New York thought. The frenzied hubbub of the business district and Wall Street are reflective of a nation, and specifically a city, that is financially wealthy but spiritually poor. "All principles," John informs his alarmed cousin, "are swallowed up in the absorbing desire for gain—national honor, permanent security, the ordinary rules of society, law, the Constitution, and everything that is usually so dear to men, are forgotten, or are perverted in order to sustain this unnatural condition of things." (p. 103) Likewise, the City's frenzied speculation in real estate has created an atmosphere of unnatural gain where even "women and clergymen are infected, and we exist under the active control of the most corrupting of all influences, 'the love of money'." (p. 105)

Needless to say, Edward is greatly disappointed by his City, his "home as found." Europe offered a culture of permanence and tradition. But the frenetic atmosphere of New York displays a hollow dynamism, a mediocrity of spirit, and a vulgar bastardization of the American ideal: "I expected to see a capital in New York," he confers with his friends while on their journey to the country estate, "and in this I have been grievously disappointed. Instead of finding the tastes, tone, conveniences, architecture, streets, churches, shops, and society of a capital, I found a huge expansion of commonplace things, a commercial town, and the most mixed and the least regulated society that I had ever met with." (p. 120)

Mr. Aristabulus Bragg, Attorney and Counsellor-at-Law, however, offers a different point of view of the City. Unlike Edward Effingham, Bragg is not a man of inherited wealth but rather a self-made success story. A poor boy from western Massachusetts who emigrated to New York, was admitted to the Bar and is now a successful "practitioner in all the courts of Otsego," Bragg, according to John Effingham, is like the City in "all that is good and all that is bad, in a very large class of . . . fellow-citizens." "He is quick-witted, prompt in action, enterprising in all things in which he has nothing to lose, but wary and cautious in all things in which he has a real stake, and ready to turn not only his hand, but his heart and his principles, to anything that offers an advantage." (p. 10)

One might easily suspect that such a character would be used by Cooper to expostulate at length on the "virtues" of the City in contrast to the negative observations of the Effingham family. But, and perhaps wisely, Cooper reduces Bragg to a mere reporter of the City's customs and beliefs. The character's own judgment is relatively non-committal and summary in form. If it were otherwise, if Bragg were to be more fully developed as a character and his views more personal, his judgments would undoubtedly rival the judgments of the Effingham's in validity and possibly reduce Cooper's intention of "educating" New Yorkers and his countrymen about their faults to a cacaphony of contrary views.

Consequently, Bragg merely tells it "like it is." He is a blunt man, and his bluntness becomes an accurate mirror of the City's characteristics. He serves yet remains aloof to its institutions. He "educates" Miss Eve about the effects of a republican government on the citizens of New York: "I do not mean that the public has a legal right to control the tastes of the citizens—but in a republican government, you undoubtedly understand, Miss Eve, it will rule in all things." (p. 14) He further warns her that her value judgments will be condemned in New York not because she is ignorant or ill-informed, but rather because she is travelled, educated, and will be criticized as anti-American in her sentiments. Turning to her friend, Grace Van Cortlandt, he jokingly amends this judgment at which "Eve smiled, for she saw that Mr. Bragg was capable of detecting and laughing at provincial pride, even while he was so much under its influence." (p. 16) Thus we encounter one example of the paradoxical City in the character of Mr. Bragg. He represents that dimension of confusion and chaos that Cooper encountered upon returning from Europe in 1833—a confusion simultaneously repugnant and attractive, dogmatic yet satirical. Indeed, in a letter to William Skinner of Baltimore in 1833, Cooper expressed his amusement upon his return at being simultaneously honored by a public dinner yet attacked by others for being pro-American! Fortunately, the City is not reflective of the nation in general, he concludes: "The heart of the nation, however, is sound, or else God knows what would become of us."[31]

Another aspect of Bragg's personality that makes him reflective of the City is that he has no roots, no traditions that govern his behavior. When questioned by a European about the lack of "local attachments," Bragg replies that "a human being is not a cat, to love a locality rather than its own interests. . . . The house I was born in was pulled down shortly after my birth, as indeed has been its successor, so I can tell you nothing on that head. . . ." (pp. 24-25)

In a similar vein, John Effingham observes later in the novel that the City and the Nation alike are perpetually in a "state of mutation," which he likens to "the game of children, in which, as one quits his corner another runs into it, and he that finds no corner to get into, is the laughing-stock of the others." (p. 118)

An amusing aside in the novel occurs with the appearance of Mr. Hammer, a real-estate auctioneer who outlines the confusing exchanges of real-estate speculation in a conversation with the Effingham family. His example is the Volkert Van Brunt farm, sold within the last two years by the sons to Peter Feeler for $5,000.00, who in turn sold it to John Search "as keen a one as we have" for $25,000.00, who then proceeded to sell it to Nathan Rise for $50,000.00 the following week, and is now offered for $112,000.00. To his astonished listeners, Hammer continues that such speculator stories are quite common in the City. "There is no calculating in the matter—for it is all fancy." (p. 101) Hammer's only regret is that the Van Brunt farm was not sooner subdivided into lots, since it would have brought a higher price and risen to its "just value" as opposed to being bought and sold at its "farm price." "Yes, sir," he informs the startled Mr. Effingham, "We have a good deal of the bottom of the sea that brings fair prices in consequence of being well mapped." (p. 102) At this point, everyone departs even more confused and undoubtedly wondering exactly what Mr. Hammer's concept of "fair prices" for under-sea real-estate actually is.

Besides the characters mentioned, Cooper introduces into the novel a host of minor characters who expand further the dimension of the City. Some of these people can be aptly classified as fools. In this category are four women—Green, Brackett, Legend, and Jarvis. Each character is a two-dimensional example of a specific form of New York habit or custom.

Mrs. Green, for example, is referred to as one of the "Hajjis," a person who sets the taste of the town. But her only qualification is that she has recently visited Paris, and from this she puts on pretensions of knowing what is in fashion. Of a similar stamp is Miss Brackett. Miss Brackett is also one of the town's moderators of taste, but her "high reputation . . . for taste and knowledge in books" has been derived from a superficial skimming of newspaper articles and journals that "do not even skim the works they pretend to analyze." (p. 49)

Mrs. Legend is an example of the pseudo-cultural elite. She is the hostess at many "literary" parties that draw upon every conceivable oddity of New York society. In Chapter Six we find her engaged in one of her dinners in which "nearly all the wits, writers, artists, and literati, as the most incorrigible members of the book clubs were styled in New York, were pressingly invited to be present." (p. 80) Furthermore, she has expanded this illustrious group by also inviting anyone conversant in foreign languages. Present are dealers in gin from Holland, a German linen merchant, and an Italian "who amused himself in selling beads." (p. 81)

Mrs. Jarvis is the last of the New York fools. She is the character type obligatory in any novel on New York—the social climber. Her husband is amusingly portrayed as a sensible fellow who tries to curb his wife's more exotic instincts, but her reasoning seems impenetrable. We find her in Chapter Four arguing with her husband, whom she feels has "so little social spirit" for the niceties of what constitutes social distinction. Her husband's reasoning ("If you wish the world to believe you the equal of any one, no matter whom, do not be always talking about it, lest they see you distrust the fact yourself." p. 45), however, fails to impress her. According to John Effingham, Mrs. Jarvis is representative of a whole new type of New Yorker—recently arrived and financially successful—that has "launched out into vulgar and uninstructed finery." (p. 51)

Such unflattering portraits of certain types of New Yorkers—and in this case all women—undoubtedly spurred criticism from some of Cooper's contemporaries that he was scornful of American women in general.[32] The charge, of course, was ridiculous. In fact, Cooper introduces two women, Mrs. Hawker and Mrs. Bloomfield, as exemplaries of the voice of reason.

Mrs. Hawker is a member of one of New York's "old families." She has little regard for such people as Mrs. Jarvis and their pretentious tomfoolery. The *noveau riche* regard her but little, and that is to her credit as John Effingham notes: "her manners would puzzle the comprehension of people whose imitation has not gone beyond the surface; and her polished and simple mind would find little sympathy among a class who seldom rise above a commonplace sentiment without getting upon stilts." (p. 51)

If Mrs. Hawker is an example of true social grace, Mrs. Bloomfield is a woman of wit and intelligence. She displays her wit in her summation of New York: "Better even than Edinburgh in many respects, and worse than Wapping in others." (p. 55) Her intelligence is evident in her caustic observation of a sycophantic

newspaper editor, Mr. Dodge: "When one betrays a profound ignorance of his own country, it is a fair presumption that he cannot
be very active in his observation of strangers." (p. 55) A regular
Benjamin Franklin in petticoats, she is a walking compendium of
similar maxims and, along with Mrs. Hawker, helps show that
Cooper is not biased in his attitude toward American women or
completely dissatisfied by the intellectual climate of New York City.
Intelligence is there, but it is overshadowed by the fools who have
temporarily made the City their own.

Such are the New Yorkers that Cooper introduces into his novel
and from which a brief outline of the City can be drawn. There are
few instances in *Home As Found* where the City becomes more of a
tangible physical presence. One is an allusion to the great fire of
1835 during which a large part of the financial district was destroyed. Cooper's account touches upon the emotions created by
the fire as well as its physical presence. In one brief passage we are
presented with an excellent description of the increasing ferocity of
the conflagration:

> They who stood the fiery masses, were freezing on one side with
> the Greenland cold of the night, while their bodies were almost
> blistered with the fierce flames on the other. There was something
> frightful in this contest of the elements, nature appearing to con-
> dense the heat within its narrowest possible limits, as if purposely
> to increase its fierceness. The effects were awful; for entire buildings
> would seem to dissolve at their touch, as the forked flames envel-
> oped them in sheets of fire. (p. 107)

It is unfortunate that such passages are not more plentiful in
Cooper's account of the City. But, on the other hand, Cooper may
have had no choice but to present the City as a collection of ideas
rather than as a physical entity. For Cooper, the City's growth due
to the likes of the Mr. Hammers was too rapid and quixotic to be
accurately delineated. The only reality was to be found in the opinions and customs of his fellow New Yorkers, and this was exactly
how home was found.

Despite its fairly short length, critics have generally considered
Herman Melville's tale, *Bartleby the Scrivener*, as being more of a
short novel than a short story. Lewis Mumford classified it as such
in 1929 when he noted that it, like the "best" short stories by

Melville, "are really short novels, while the lesser ones . . . are little more than mediocre anecdotes."[33] Raymond Weaver also classified the story as a novel when he included it in his anthology, *Shorter Novels of Herman Melville*, a tradition that has persisted to the present day as witnessed in its inclusion in the modern Bantam paperback edition of *Herman Melville's Four Short Novels*.

What has undoubtedly made critics so favorable to addressing *Bartleby* as a novel lies in its amazingly compact and detailed development of character. Bartleby and the narrator, who remains nameless throughout the story, are so carefully delineated yet paradoxically ambiguous that they have become the source material for many an article on the tale. Much has been said about the possible influences of Melville's background on the plot development, and for Melville scholars the comparison between the narrator with Melville's own father-in-law, Judge Lemuel Shaw, goes without saying. Shaw's frequent offers of financial assistance to the young writer and his new wife are quite similar to the narrator's expedient, albeit helpful, offers of money to Bartleby. Furthermore, Melville's own resistance to the "kind advice" of his friends and relations to pattern his fiction after the more popular examples of the day ring similar to Bartleby's persistent rejection of the narrator's "reasonable" directives.

But it is dangerous to assume that herein lies the sole concern, the entire focus of Melville's story—namely that he is involved in some extensive cathartic process whereby he can expunge all his innermost animosities towards well-meaning friends. Freudians aside, the story is, after all, primarily a portrait of New York City as the subtitle, *a tale of Wall Street*, clearly implies.

As a born and bred New Yorker, Melville well knew the City. Despite his extended journeys at sea and his temporary life as a gentleman farmer in Pittsfield, Massachusetts, he would spend more than half of his life within the City's boundaries and eventually die there, virtually unknown to his contemporaries. Furthermore, despite his reputation as the man who had "lived among the cannibals" in the South Pacific, Melville was preeminently a New Yorker exhibiting all the ambivalence and pent-up frustration of any New Yorker trying to come to grips with his City. As a gentleman farmer in Massachusetts, we find him composing letters to his New York friends decrying the "heat and dust of the Babylonish brick-kiln of New York."[34] Yet despite these reveries, his family would return to the City in about ten years, having found country living more than their health could bear. Melville's recurrent bouts with sciatica made pushing a plow torturous, and his wife hated the harsh Pittsfield winters.

Back in the City, Melville settled into a rather comfortable position as a district inspector of customs for New York Harbor and an uneventful life marred principally by increasing domestic troubles with his wife and children. At home, Melville became increasingly silent and withdrawn, taking on the personality of his character Bartleby and unnerving his wife to such an extent that she actively sought a divorce. Yet another side of Melville is witnessed by his friends, who see in him a "proud, shy, sensitively honorable" man carrying out his uneventful duties as a customs inspector, confused and baffled by the aberrent behavior of his son Stanwix and seemingly accidental death of his other son Malcolm.[35] In this light, Melville is not unlike the confused and essentially humane narrator of our tale. Ironically, it is a case of life imitating art since the story had already been composed ten years prior to Melville's return to the City. Therefore, what becomes particularly intriguing is how closely the characters encompass the full spectrum of human behavior as witnessed in Melville's own family and, as such, they are reflective of the City in general.

The successful New Yorker, the contented New Yorker, the conservative and confident New Yorker—the Melville at the customs house—is portrayed in the narrator. His self-portrait, with which the story begins, points to a man whose principal virtue, as he sees it, is his being a "safe" man. The term is obviously ironic, since it refers to not only the narrator's eminently cautious business practices but to the fact that he is often responsible for large sums of money that pass through the doors of his Wall Street law firm. In short, he *is* a safe with the same stolidity and reliability of a bank vault. He revels in the trust the late John Jacob Astor placed in him: "a name which, I admit, I love to repeat, for it hath a rounded and obicular sound to it, and rings like unto bullion,"[36] and reflects throughout the story on the economic viability of those under his employ as a way of determining their intrinsic worth. Thus under the surface of a seemingly convivial nature prone to accept without too much questioning the apparent vagaries of his employees—Turkey, Nippers, Ginger Nut, and, of course, Bartleby—there lies a steeled soul that tolerates eccentricity

21

only so far as it does not interfere with the economics of good business. He accepts Turkey's emotional outbursts only because they occur during the afternoon hours, whereas those of Nippers "were mainly observable in the morning." "Their fits relieved each other, like guards," he applauds. "When Nippers's was on, Turkey's was off and *vice versa*. This was a good natural arrangement, under the circumstances." (p. 9)

It is therefore imperative not to be fooled by the narrator's *professed* humanity or apparent concern for others nor confused by the subtle humor that Melville injects into this tragic tale about isolation and suffering. These are merely masks of the true City and its inhabitants of which the narrator represents the most successful. His tolerance and concern for Bartleby are contingent upon the scrivener's industry—in spite of his eccentricities:

> As days passed on, I became considerably reconciled to Bartleby. His steadiness, his freedom from all dissipation, his incessant industry (except when he chose to throw himself into a standing reverie behind his screen), his great stillness, his unalterableness of demeanor under all circumstances, made him a valuable acquisition. (p. 18)

As soon as Bartleby's behavior begins to influence profits, however, the narrator finds himself in a dilemma. His better self pleads for a moral responsibility to Bartleby, but business ethics, the part of him that has been nurtured by the City and dictated by "the constant friction of illiberal minds," as our narrator puts it, "wears out at last the best resolves of the more generous." (p. 31) Such protestations, however, strike a somewhat hollow note coming from him. His generosity is, after all, the generosity of the City—it can only exist within economic parameters. When he finally leaves Bartleby at the Tombs, he tries to pay off his guilt by offering Bartleby some money: "But it dropped upon the floor. . . ." (p. 34)

Yet it is not Melville's intention to cast the narrator solely as a villain, coldly and heartlessly rejecting Bartleby's need for compassion. The narrator's dilemma lies in the dichotomy of his character. One half sympathizes with Bartleby and makes it difficult to completely forget the scrivener. When the narrator parts from Bartleby, he simultaneously longs for and fears departure. "I tore myself from him whom I had so longed to be rid of." (p. 34) This is the narrator's humane side, and it is frequently expressed in other sentiments as when he earlier speaks of charity as a "great safe-guard" to its possessor: "Men have committed murder for jealousy's sake, and anger's sake, and hatred's sake, and selfishness' sake, and spiritual pride's sake; but no man, that ever I heard of, ever committed a diabolical murder for sweet charity's sake." (p. 30)

Such statements can be easily applauded, but at their core they nevertheless seem to ring of sententiousness—as though our narrator were bent upon parroting the prudence of a successful businessman. In short, his words are belied by his actions; his deeds outweigh his sentiments no matter how noble they may be.

The reason for this lies in the fact that the dominant half of the narrator's character is that which has been completely absorbed by the City. On practically every page the narrator is presented as a man whose whole identity and consciousness is mandated by this environment, ironically, even more so than Bartleby's. For example, the narrator is a firm believer in environmental determinism; free will has little play in his scheme of things. New Yorkers are like their City; they fall into the regularity of the Wall Street environment from which there is no escape. Turkey and Nippers exhibit their characteristic behaviors in a highly predictable manner, and the narrator is convinced that diet and digestion play an important role in their personalities. According to him, Nippers is cantankerous in the morning due to indigestion, a state that fades as the day continues. Turkey's physical condition is likewise predetermined by similar external stimuli.

Understandably the narrator finds himself completely baffled by the unpredictability of Bartleby. Bartleby's diet consists entirely of gingernuts, but his personality exhibits none of the traits of the spicy food: "Now, what was ginger? A hot, spicy thing. Was Bartleby hot and spicy? Not at all. Ginger, then, had no effect upon Bartleby. Probably he preferred it should have none," he concludes. (p. 15) The narrator also finds himself unable to counteract the unpredictableness of Bartleby. At first he is confused by Bartleby's refusal to read legal documents. But as the story progresses and Bartleby's withdrawal becomes more complete, the narrator's confusion evolves into a physical-emotional paralysis. He is unable to call the police to remove Bartleby from the offices, yet deplores the scrivener's "cadaverous triumph." (p. 29) He finds himself wandering aimlessly in the streets, examining and questioning every avenue of response but unable to act on any. Every attempt on the part of the narrator to argue with Bartleby "according to common usage and common sense" fails miserably. (p. 13) Every attempt to come to grips with Bartleby's strange behavior is fruitless. The narrator tries to classify Bartleby first as eccentric, then as disturbed and even considers the possibility of Bartleby's being homicidal, but each consideration proves false. In the end the narrator is as immobile as the scrivener. He applies every technique he knows as a New Yorker to the dilemma and fails terribly because Bartleby's behavior lies outside the understanding of the typical urban consciousness used to the unhindered routines of daily city life. Bartleby represents the eccentric, the aberrant, that the average New Yorker prefers to ignore, buried in his morning newspaper, rushing to his job or next appointment.

Nor is the narrator alone in his dilemma. When in desperation he retreats to new offices in order to free himself from his nemesis, he soon learns that Bartleby's strange behavior and refusal to leave the old building on Wall Street has put everyone there in an uproar. "Everybody is concerned," the landlord informs him, "clients are leaving the offices; some fears are entertained of a mob. . . ." (p. 35) In fact, so disturbing is the strange behavior of Bartleby, that the narrator finds solace only by retreating into the everyday noise and din of the Manhattan streets, streets whose normal excitement are comforting to a mind shocked by the unnerving quiet of Bartleby.

Yet Bartleby is not totally alien to the City. Unlike the narrator, he represents a different perspective of it. He is more expressive of the passive City—the physical, concrete world of Wall Street on a Sunday afternoon in conflict with the active, human City of the weekday, represented more by the narrator. This is an important distinction to make because it amends the traditional manner of characterizing Bartleby as a "failure" or outsider in a City that cannot understand him. True, he is an outsider within the active City, but in his own realm of the passive City—the City without humanity—he is eminently successful; so successful, indeed, that his entire personality merges with the brick walls outside the law office and later with the stone walls of the Tombs.

It seems to be Melville's intention, therefore, not to portray the outcast, such as the artist or creative person (like Melville) at odds with an insensitive, unfeeling mercantile-oriented city. Rather, it is the author's intention to show how far the New Yorker could change under the influence of his environment, until his entire personality merges with the empty physical entity of the City.

There is no conceivable way that Bartleby can be misconstrued as an artist; his initial productivity in the story is entirely uncreative, and as far as the narrator is concerned, highly indispensible. His output is extraordinary as is the quality of his copy. "As if long famished for something to copy," the narrator applauds, "he seemed to gorge on my documents. There was no pause for digestion. He ran a day and night line, copying by sunlight and by candle-light." (p. 11) This is not the production of a creative mind. The personality does not obtrude here in any way. Instead we are confronted by the output of a machine—like a modern-day photocopier—that reproduces documents, as does Bartleby, "silently, palely, mechanically." (p. 11)

Nor in Bartleby's rebellion is there the slightest element of personality, of an individual speaking out in protest against an unfeeling world. Instead we are confronted with a "malfunction" of sorts of an otherwise highly effective working machine. Consequently, Bartleby's rebellion fails to elicit an angry response from the narrator. As Bartleby's "malfunction" increases in scope and seriousness, the narrator experiences the emotions of incredulity, amazement, frustration, and even irritability—but never anger. He finds it impossible to be angry with Bartleby (at least on a one-to-one human basis) because of the scrivener's totally unemotional statement: "I would prefer not to."

> I looked at him steadfastly. His face was leanly composed; his grey eye dimly calm. Not a wrinkle of agitation rippled him. Had there been the least uneasiness, anger, impatience or impertinence in his manner; in other words, had there been anything ordinarily human about him, doubtless I should have violently dismissed him from the premises. But as it was, I should have as soon thought of turning my pale plaster-of-paris bust of Cicero out of doors. (p. 12)

It is this emotionless aspect of Bartleby that is crucial in understanding him as a character. In Melville's New York landscape, it is emotion that determines the intrinsic human qualities of the characters. Despite their being victims of habits and rituals, the other scriveners in the law office are prone to emotional outbursts; only each has his own particular outburst at different times during the workday. Thus Nippers' dyspeptic personality is active in the morning, while the "fine florid hue" of Turkey blazes "like a grate full of Christmas coals" during the afternoon hours. (p. 5) These are their specifically human characteristics—predictable as they may be. Bartleby, on the other hand, lacks these emotional traits and is instead as emotionless and as passive as his work environment.

His desk is nestled into a corner of the office bordered with a high green folding screen (with which the narrator can isolate Bartleby for privacy) and a windowed wall once presenting "a lateral view of certain grimy backyards and bricks, but which, owing to subsequent erections, commanded at present no view at all. . . ." (p. 10) Within his niche Bartleby becomes the epitome of the "company man," devoid of questions or ideas, staring for long periods when not at work out of his "pale window behind the screen, upon the dead brick wall." (p. 21) He even takes up residence in the law offices and seems to exist within their confines without food, drawing his sustenance from the atmosphere around him. One Sunday when the narrator accidently stumbles upon Bartleby's presence in the offices, he is shocked by the terrible isolation evident in the scrivener's retreat from society:

> Immediately then the thought came sweeping across me, what miserable friendlessness and loneliness are here revealed! His poverty is great; but his solitude, how horrible! Think of it. On a Sunday, Wall Street is deserted as Petra; and every night of every day it is an emptiness. This building, too, which of week-days hums with industry and life, at nightfall echoes with sheer vacancy, and all through Sunday is forlorn. And here Bartleby makes his home; sole spectator of a solitude which he has seen all populous—a sort of innocent and transformed Marius brooding among the ruins of Carthage! (p. 20)

By the end of the tale, Bartleby has become so absorbed by his environment, he cannot exist outside of it and dies when finally removed to the Tombs where our narrator last sees him "in the quietest of the yards, his face towards a high wall." (p. 38)

Unlike the law offices, nature has made a foothold within the very depths of this prison and a "soft imprisoned turf" is growing underfoot, as if "by some strange magic, through the clifts, grass-seed, dropped by birds, had sprung." (p. 40) This natural world is what the narrator feels will restore Bartleby within the oppressive man-made environment of the Tombs. "Look," he optimistically exclaims to Bartleby, "there is the sky, and here is the grass." But this is a human response. Bartleby can only reply, "I know where I am," and remain unmoved. (pp. 38-39) What the narrator cannot understand is that it is the deserted canyons of Wall Street and not Nature that Bartleby craves. Outside his *natural* milieu he can no longer exist and dies, "his knees, drawn up . . . lying on his side, his head touching the cold stones. . . ." (p. 40) "Ah, Bartleby! Ah, humanity!" solidifies Melville's distressing theme of the City, as well as the narrator's final awareness that man, in his quest for civilization, has simultaneously created the very monuments to his self-destruction.

Chapter One

[1]Edward Robb Ellis, *The Epic of New York City* (New York: Coward-McCann, Inc., 1966), p. 228.

[2]*Ibid.*, p. 223.

[3]Bayrd Still, *Mirror for Gotham: New York As Seen By Contemporaries from Dutch Days to the Present* (New York: New York University Press, 1956), p. 84.

[4]Allan Nevins, ed., *The Diary of Philip Hone 1828-1851* (New York: Dodd, Mead & Company, 1936), p. 148.

[5]*Ibid.*, p. 151.

[6]Still, p. 88.

[7]p. 79.

[8]p. 127.

[9]p. 174.

[10]Ellis, p. 250.

[11]p. 250.

[12]Still, p. 142.

[13]Nevins, p. 609.

[14]Still, p. 92.

[15]p. 134.

[16]p. 141.

[17]Nevins, p. 41.

[18]Ellis, p. 273.

[19]Still, p. 80.

[20]Still, p. 99.

[21]Louis Untermeyer, ed., *The Poetry and Prose of Walt Whitman* (New York: Simon and Schuster, 1949), pp. 868-69.

[22]Nevins, p. 772.

[23]Still, p. 202.

[24]pp. 114-15.

[25]p. 142.

[26]Untermeyer, p. 814.

[27]Donald A. Ringe, *James Fenimore Cooper* (New York: Twayne, 1962), p. 12.

[28]*Ibid*. p. 74.

[29]James Fenimore Cooper, *Home As Found* (1838; rpt. New York: G.P. Putnam's Sons, ND), p. iv; henceforth all future references to this book will be followed with the page number(s).

[30]Dorothy Waples, *The Whig Myth of James Fenimore Cooper* (1938; rpt. New York: Archon Books, 1968), p. 213.

[31]James Fenimore Cooper, ed., *Correspondence of James Fenimore Cooper* (New Haven: Yale University Press, 1922), II, 328.

[32]Waples, pp. 217-18.

[33]Lewis Mumford, "Melville's Miserable Year," in *Bartleby the Inscrutable*, ed. M. Thomas Inge (Hamden, Conn.: Archon Books, 1979), p. 58.

[34]Merrell R. Davis, ed., *The Letters of Herman Melville* (New Haven: Yale University Press, 1960), p. 132.

[35]Tyrus Hillway, *Herman Melville* (Boston: Twayne, 1979), p. 64.

[36]Herman Melville, "Bartleby," in *Four Short Novels by Herman Melville*, ed. William Plomer (1946; rpt. New York: Bantam Books, Inc., 1971), p. 4; henceforth all future references to this book will be followed with the page number(s).

CHAPTER II

The Polarized City:
Edith Wharton's *House of Mirth*
and Stephen Crane's *Maggie*

By the end of the nineteenth century, New York City was no longer struggling for an identity. Along with its physical and economic growth, there had developed a personality, a way of life, that made New York different from other American and European cities. Two major influences responsible for this change were the rising immigrant population during the 1890's and the increasing power of Wall Street. These factors not only made the City unique but permeated and polarized every facet of city life, clearly dividing the rich from the poor. Thus were found in lower Manhattan the tenement slums whose seething humanity and wretched poverty contrasted sharply with the elegant baronial mansions of the elite on Fifth Avenue. Nothing more startled the visitor to New York at the turn of the century than this contrast.

In their works on New York City, Edith Wharton and Stephen Crane deal with this dualistic City, but rather than examine the contrast between the rich and the poor in its entirety, they focus instead on one end of the spectrum—Wharton with the rich and Crane with the poor. This was essential because a sweeping, all-encompassing overview would have been impossible, given the fact that a substantial middle-class had yet to be formed and would not be clearly defined until the 1920's. Without this middle ground to act as a link between the two extremes, the focus of each novel would have been too clearly divided. Instead, the novelists portray the ends of the spectrum they know best and can write about effectively.

In dealing with the rich, Wharton examines a way of life she lived. Born into a family of wealthy New York merchants, bankers, and lawyers, and educated by tutors and governesses, she knew high society—its glittering extremes and its pitfalls. In *The House of Mirth*, which appeared in 1905 and established her reputation as a writer, she deals with this world. Crane, on the other hand, was unfamiliar with the details of high society. A newspaperman, he had a nose for the lurid and the bizarre, and nothing could have been more lurid and bizarre than the slums of lower Manhattan in the 1890's. Having lived in the slums for some time, Crane composed his novelette, *Maggie: A Girl of the Streets*, an expose of the conditions of poverty and its influence on people, in 1893. Interestingly, despite the opposite focus of each writer, their conclusions are surprisingly similar. New York as a socially polarized city is an unhealthy city for, as in Edith Wharton's novel, the inhabitants live out their lives in insulated, greedy splendor, or as in Crane's, they end up as drunkards and prostitutes. Without the middle-class, there is no middle ground, no salvation, for this seemingly invincible metropolis at the turn of the century.

A visitor to the City during these times could form an opinion about the rich by simply observing the buildings in which they lived and worked. The mansions of the rich on Fifth Avenue above 49th Street were truly grandiose and represented practically every architectural style imaginable as each merchant attempted to excel his neighbor in magnificence and splendor. William K. Vanderbilt commissioned the famous architect, Richard Morris Hunt, to build a "French chateau" that would rival the grandeur of the Medici mansions of Florence. Replicas of the ancestral homes of European nobility were the order of the day, and the Vanderbilt mansion competed for attention with the cream-colored Touraine Chateau at the northeast corner of 56th Street built by William Waldorf Astor. Nearby the ominous gray stone palazzo of Collis P. Huntington, the California railroad magnet, loomed majestically on 57th Street.

The interiors of these mansions were as magnificent as their exteriors. The Vanderbilt mansion boasted a reception hall larger than the Supreme Court of the United States, a high grand salon, and an immense ballroom which could also double as a private theatre. Huntington installed in his red-brocaded drawing room an adjustable easy chair, controlled by levers, in which he could easily contemplate his Vermeers and Rembrandts. Other mansions were similarly adorned, and it was not uncommon to find the art treasures of Europe in many. The Madison Avenue mansion of Henry

O. Havemeyer boasted no less than seven Rembrandts. William Whitney's residence was accessible through gates taken from the Palazzo Doria in Rome, and its Gargantuan ballroom was from a castle in Bordeaux. Other mansions were decorated with the spoils of the East as well as Europe. Stained-glass windows from French monasteries, frescoes from the palaces of Genoese and Roman princes, Persian rugs, Flemish tapestries, Chinese porcelain, historic furniture, illuminated manuscripts, and Renaissance gold work—all found their way into the mansions of the rich where they testified to the wealth of their owners.

But it was not only the homes of the wealthy that reflected such power; the commercial buildings of lower Manhattan also echoed this prosperity. Architectural daring predominated, and some of the most stately business buildings caused as many a raised eyebrow as the palaces of upper Fifth Avenue. The Tower Building at 50 Broadway was one such structure. Built in 1885, the architect, Bradford Lee Gilbert, was labeled a madman for proposing to raise his structure to a daring thirteen stories on a framework of steel rather than the usual stone. The concept was so revolutionary that many feared the building would soon collapse, and nearby merchants vacated their premises. Nevertheless, the architect claimed that his building could withstand a 100 mile per hour gale, and indeed when an 80 mile per hour wind did hit the City in 1886, crowds gathered to see the building collapse. It did not, however. A daring Gilbert even climbed to the tenth story of the unfinished building and dropped a plumb-line to test its soundness; not a vibration was detected. Such fanfare made the Tower Building one of the most sought-after business addresses in New York City—for a while. In 1913 it was torn down to make way for even more daring and controversial designs.

Building codes had been revised and architects were now given almost a free rein. Bruce Price designed the twenty-story American Surety Company, claimed to be the City's first real skyscraper. Then came the St. Paul Building, which rose twenty-five stories. Before long "skyscrapers" became a common word in the New Yorker's lexicon, and the City took on the appearance of a mythical kingdom of giants.

Such grandeur served as a reflection of how the rich viewed itself. In a sense, the building became an extension of an egotistical self-image. Such vanity naturally had other outlets, the most notable being the grand parties the wealthy always seemed to be attending. Giving a grand party often became the principal function among many of these people, and they were never simple forms of entertainment. They too became testimonials of wealth and power, where families could parade their glittering jewelry and costumes before an astonished America.

One of the major haunts of New York's high society was the newly built Waldorf-Astoria. It hosted in 1897 one of the most extravagant parties ever given—the Bradley-Martin Ball. At the time the Nation was experiencing a serious financial depression; businesses were going bankrupt and many people were out of work. Mrs. Martin ignored the times and decided that what New York truly needed was an elegant ball. She sent out 1,200 invitations for a costume ball and requested guests to dress themselves for Versailles during the reign of Louis XV.

Rumors abounded during the week before the prospective ball. One claimed that over a quarter million dollars had been spent. The unemployed in the City were unamused, and on the night of the ball a large squad of police were detailed to protect the participants from possible mob violence. Other rumors circulated that anarchists would plant bombs on the ground floor, and the windows were boarded up ostensibly to ward off the curious.

Contrary to suspicions, as the guests arrived, a peaceful crowd gathered to see the splendid display of opulence. One guest entered wearing a suit of steel armor inlaid with gold and costing (one newspaper account breathlessly noted) ten thousand dollars. Of the many notables invited, seven hundred attended, and according to Frederick Townsend Martin, brother of the host, " 'The power of wealth with its refinement and vulgarity, was everywhere . . . in many cases the diamond buttons worn by the men represented thousands of dollars, and the value of the historical gems worn by the ladies baffled description.' "[1] During the course of the festivities over sixty-one cases each of champaigne and wine were consumed, along with five hundred bottles of mineral water. The party was an immense success; in fact, it was so splendid that New York City doubled the tax assessment of the Martin's who, as a result, moved to England. Such was the price that had to be paid for giving an elegant ball so like, as one newspaper account noted, "a stately court function in one of the capitals of Europe."[2]

Not all parties had the elegance of the Bradley-Martin affair, but some did exceed it in vulgarity. One such party was given for

"Diamond" Jim Brady by Stanford White, the famous architect, in White's studio high in the tower of Madison Square Garden. Story has it that when dessert was to be served, waiters brought out an immense Jack Horner pie which was set on the table. A red ribbon was given to Brady and white ones to each of the other guests and the host. When the ribbons were pulled a beautiful, naked girl arose from the pie, with Brady's red ribbon attached to her arm. Brady, of course, reeled her in. So as not to disappoint the other guests who were left holding the white ribbons attached to nothing, White clapped his hands and eleven naked women entered from surrounding doors and jumped into the laps of the company. In its way, Brady's party was as successful, albeit more scandalous, than the Bradley-Martin Ball.

Of course the amusements of the rich were not limited to grandiose parties. Wealth was flaunted in many ways. Gambling became a popular diversion. One notorious millionaire, John W. Gates, known by his friends as "bet a million," enjoyed gambling on anything from horses to stock markets, or even the progress of two raindrops down a windowpane. During one baccarat game with his friends, which ended at five in the morning, more than one million dollars changed hands.

A number of illicit gambling places catered to people like Gates and his rich friends. One was Frank Farrell's near the Waldorf Hotel on 33rd Street. This place was frequented by the previously noted "Diamond" Jim Brady. The interior was designed by Stanford White at a cost of five hundred thousand dollars and boasted a massive Italian Renaissance bronze door at the rear of the entrance hall. The finest cigars, wines, and liquors were available to the patrons for free, and it was said that at least fifty thousand dollars were exchanged each night with some of the wins well over the two hundred thousand dollar mark. Another casino run by Richard Canfield was also very popular. A Sybarite's delight, it had an interior costing over one million dollars. Private rooms were available for those who wished to exceed the limits of the house, the highest of any casino in the world, and over five hundred thousand dollars were kept in its vault each night. Admission was highly limited, with players expected to purchase a minimum of five hundred dollars in chips. If a patron refused, he was respectfully told not to return.

Besides gambling and parties, the rich took their pleasure in a myriad of other ways. There were the yachting and automobile clubs that sponsored yearly rallies and exhibitions where proud owners could show off their new White Steamer, imported Mercedes or Peugeot. The first event of the winter season was the celebrated annual horse show. English experts were even exported as judges, and boxes cost more than four hundred dollars. Bicycling was also a popular sport among the wealthy. "Diamond" Jim gave Lillian Russell a gold-plated, jewel-studded Royale and had a dozen gilded ones made for himself. Finally, there were the eating places, such as Delmonico's, Sherry's, Rectors (popular with the after-theatre crowd), and, of course, the Waldorf's exclusive Palm Room that required formal attire (white tie and tail for gentlemen and evening gowns for ladies). Waiters had to be conversant in French and German and had to be clean-shaven. Exotic fare included green turtle soup, roast of mountain sheep with puree of chestnuts, diamond-back terrapin, and ruddy duck. No wonder the chef made ten thousand dollars a year, a salary so high for its day that it was questioned in domestic and foreign newspapers. Such was the life of the rich—complacent, happy, vain, arrogant, searching for its own pleasure and ignorant of the suffering around it.

If the rich cared little about the conditions of the poor, the poor certainly knew nothing about the lifestyle of the rich. Slum life was not in a sense a life but rather a form of existence, a way of coping against immeasurable odds and hardships for a piece of the American dream, and for many that piece was very, very small. While the millions of immigrants who poured into New York City at the turn of the century found freedom from the political or religious persecution of a European nobility, they could not anticipate the persecution they would now face in their adopted land as a result of their being foreign and poor. Forced into their respective tenement districts of lower Manhattan, the population density grew at such an alarming rate that there were nearly one thousand persons per acre in lower Manhattan. Apartments herded nine to fifteen people per room, and in one downtown block 2,781 people scratched out a miserable existence.

If the rich grew richer day by day, it was because they paid their workers starvation wages. Without union or governmental restraints, the capitalists ruled the Nation on their own terms, and the terms were harsh. Child labor was mandatory in many families where the father's salary could barely take care of himself and his wife. Many children worked at home making garments, cigars, or artificial flowers at twenty cents a gross.

With luck a child could survive, but the monotonous, unhealthy indoor work was not a good substitute for play. Still, it was better than abandonment. Danish-born Jacob Riis recorded with his camera the plight of these children in their tenements. He described one case of a foundling whose parent had written on a slip of paper, "Take care of Johnny, for God's sake. I cannot."[3] By 1889 the Children's Aid Society had sheltered some three hundred thousand outcast, orphaned children. Lewis Hine of Wisconsin documented similar conditions with his camera, most notably the case of a seven-year-old girl whose legs had become paralyzed from sitting cross-legged for four years pulling basting threads.

Uninterested in the homes or places of business of the rich, Riis and Hine recorded instead the environment of the poor. The sunless courts of tenement buildings cross-hatched with the day's wash, the swarming, impassable streets of the lower East Side where every kind of article, fresh or otherwise, could be bargained for, the back alleys with the members of a local street gang poised behind ashcans—all were recorded. Here there were no mansions boasting the artwork or architecture of European palaces. Instead were found buildings of rickety construction, too few fire escapes, inadequate plumbing, and poor light. The squeaking water pump down the hallway shared by many tenants became, as Riis noted, "the lullaby of the tenement-house babes."[4] Apartments had few furnishings. Among them was the indispensable coal stove used for both cooking and heating, but also emitting noxious fumes and coal dust that permeated every corner. Under these conditions life was hard, brutal, and very short. Less than one in five children reached maturity.

Unlike the rich, the poor had little time for amusement. Working from twelve to eighteen hours a day left one disinclined for diversions. Nevertheless, the poor areas of the City had their own unique forms of entertainment. There were the East Side Cafes where intellectuals gathered to discuss radical politics and social reform. Among them could be found Emma Goldman, a short, stocky, plain woman whose philosophical anarchism earned her the nickname of "Red Emma," and Alexander Berkman, Emma's lover, who attempted to assassinate Carnegie's partner, Henry Clay Frick, during the Homestead Strike. There were the ethnic theatres where such performers as the Jewish comedians Weber and Fields regaled hundreds, and Jacob Adler played a memorable Shylock. There were the nickleodeons where moving pictures were shown in separate machines for a dime—the cheapest amusement for the poor. Outside these establishments brilliant posters advertised the adventure and excitement within. Finally there were the dance halls and saloons (the habitues of street gangs) which were frequently condemned by clergymen and reformers for breeding criminal behavior and encouraging prostitution.

One such clergyman, Dr. Parkhurst, of the Madison Square Presbyterian Church and President of the Society for the Prevention of Crime, went undercover with a police guide to report meaningfully on the depravity of the slums. Attired in a dirty shirt, a pair of loud, black-and-white trousers, and a tie from the sleeve of an old red flannel shirt, the doctor visited saloons, brothels and gambling dens. In a particularly notorious house for homosexual prostitution, he encountered young boys in cubicles who dressed and behaved like young girls and called each other by women's names. Such scandalous conditions were later reported by Parkhurst to his congregation and the press, but reforms were few in coming since many of the establishments he abhorred were receiving protection from the police and politicians for a fee.

Saloons and alcoholism were another serious problem in the slums. Temperance movements waged annual battles against saloons that seemed to get richer every year. One, The Silver Dollar, opposite the Essex Market Court, had one thousand silver dollars embedded in the floor, a chandelier sparkling with five hundred silver dollars, and a large star and crescent behind the bar similarly decorated. One of the most infamous Bowery dives was McGurk's, also known as "Suicide Hall," a combination saloon, brothel, and meeting place for thieves and riff-raff. Murders were frequent.

Such conditions outraged many decent New Yorkers and made it even more difficult for the poor to rise above their station in life. But widespread corruption within the City government and the fact that a good percentage of the saloons and slum real estate were owned by the wealthy who had political pull precluded permanent reforms. In 1897, Asa Bird Gardiner became the new Attorney General. He provided a slogan that swept the City: "To hell with reform." And his sentiments were echoed by many who similarly chanted, "Well, well, reform has gone to hell," thereby permanently maintaining the status quo.[5]

In *The House of Mirth*, Edith Wharton does not present any constructive plan of reform. Instead, she focuses on the monied world of luxury and elegance and its influence on, and eventual destruction of, the heroine, Lily Bart, the beautiful and intelligent but poor relation of a wealthy aunt. Lily's world is one where money rules every aspect of society and is frequently capable of debasing both people and ideals. It is a world where even New York City becomes a metaphysical symbol of this hidden ugliness. When Lawrence Seldon, a lawyer and close friend of Lily, unexpectedly encounters her at Grand Central Station on a hot summer day, he is startled that she should appear in the City at a time when most everyone with means has escaped to the country. Lily's reason for being in the City is not clear, but more important is the fact that the City weighs down upon her with its oppressive heat and ugliness. Her eyes "despairingly" scan the "dreary thoroughfare" before the Station; she is annoyed that in summer "New York seems to sit in its shirtsleeves."[6] In winter, it presents an "interminable perspective of snow-burdened days," while its springs are filled with "raw sunshine and furious air." (p. 190) These negative images are further compounded when she experiences personal loss. Deprived of her aunt's inheritance, her future stretches before her "dull and bare as the deserted length of Fifth Avenue . . ." (p. 240); later reduced to making a meager living at a milliner's, we see her in the evening trudging "westward through the dreary March twilight toward the street where her boardinghouse stood." (p. 297) When dismissed from the milliner's the City's sky looms cold and gray, and a furious wind spirals dust up and down the street and against her face. Indeed, the only time the City becomes cheerful is during the last chapter after she dies from an overdose of sedatives:

> The next morning rose mild and bright, with a promise of summer in the air. The sunlight slanted joyously down Lily's street, mellowed the blistered house-front, gilded the paintless railings of the door-step, and struck prismatic glories from the panes of her darkened window. (p. 337)

Thus the City environment is naturally cruel, a personified demon that shares in the destruction of innocents like Lily Bart. But Wharton, of course, is not intent on merely revealing New York City as a vile place without redeeming qualities. Her intention is to focus on it as the center of a deterministic universe.

Success in *The House of Mirth* is merely another form of survival in the economic jungle of New York City. Economic determinism guides the characters in this novel. Surrounded by the rich and powerful, Lily soon learns that money brings with it an almost invincible power, but a power that crushes and subverts the finer instincts in man. Justice, honor, courage, love—all are sacrificed in the search for wealth and a false security against poverty and lonliness.

Although not independently wealthy, Lily was once a member of the moderately well-to-do, but the bankruptcy of her father has left her at loose ends, circulating among the rich, attending their parties, and assisting hostesses. For Lawrence Seldon she appears to "have cost a great deal to make, that a great deal of dull and ugly people must, in some mysterious way, have been sacrificed to produce her." (p. 7) At this point in her life she reflects the grandeur of the society she frequents. Her opinions, dress, and even to a certain extent her beauty, are derived from it, and as such, she shares, or so it seems to Seldon, in the collective guilt of a society that derives its elegance from the toil and suffering of the poor and helpless. Thus at the beginning Wharton sets the tone of the novel; the heartlessness of a raw, unrestrained capitalism is immediately exposed and questioned. The tragedy, however, is that Seldon sees only the exterior of Lily; her intrinsic kindness goes undetected and eventually results in her downfall within the society of which she has tried so hard to be a part.

Simon Rosedale, however, is a true representative of economic determinism in New York society. Rosedale, despised and loathed by the wealthy around him because he is a Jew, nevertheless rises within the course of the novel to become the most economically powerful of Lily's acquaintances. In essence, he is a contrasting parallel of Lily, for her failure and ostracism accompanies his rise in society until he becomes at the end a "figure on municipal committees and charitable boards." (p. 249) No longer an outcast, he has joined the ranks of those who once scorned him. Wealth has given him the power to do this; it is the principal determiner of acceptance within the City.

On another level is Bertha Dorset, a philandering wife who wrongly slanders Lily as an adulteress so as to avoid detection in her own extramarital affairs. Bertha becomes Lily's nemesis in the novel, persecuting her until the end, and she succeeds because of her wealth. Her social credit is based on an "impregnable bank-account" that Lily cannot hope to rival. Once again, success is determined by the economic power of the individual.

The City as part of a deterministic universe, however, is found on all socio-economic levels. When Lily is reduced to having to work in a milliner's shop, she soon discovers that survival here too is difficult. Ignorant of specific skills, she encounters in the milliner's shop the same cold, deterministic world she did amidst the rich. Lily is again as out of place as she was in the baronial estates of her former friends. She assumes at first that she is her co-workers' superior; that somehow her familiarity with the upper classes endows her with a special "deftness of touch." But after two months she still finds herself unable to shape or trim hats, much to the amusement of her fellow workers and the chagrin of the forewoman. An outcast of the society that nurtured her, Lily painfully realizes that she can never compete with professional ability:

> She had learned by experience that she had neither the aptitude nor the moral constancy to remake her life on new lines, to become a worker among workers and let the world of luxury and pleasure sweep by her unregarded. She could not hold herself much to blame for this ineffectiveness, and she was perhaps less to blame than she believed. Inherited tendencies had combined with early training to make her the highly specialized product she was: an organism as helpless out of its narrow range as the sea-anemone torn from the rock. She had been fashioned to adorn and delight; to what other end does nature round the rose leaf and paint the hummingbird's breast? And was it her fault that the purely decorative mission is less easily and harmoniously fulfilled among social beings than in the world of nature? That it is apt to be hampered by material necessities or complicated by moral scruples? (p. 311)

Lily's failure, therefore, is due to her being trapped within her own class. And when she can no longer succeed in it, she must fail on the lower rungs of society since she lacks the prerequisites of a skilled worker.

She contemplates the success of other "self-made women" but fails to realize that they originated on lower levels and moved up the social ladder as did Rosedale. Lily lacks the sharp-wittedness that this type of life demands; nor does she have the means to stand apart from her surroundings. She derives so much of her self-image from her environment that it becomes a reflection of her inner sense of worth or lack of it. Surrounded by elegance, she becomes elegant, as she does at the Trenors. But when confined later to the dinginess of a boardinghouse, she in turn becomes dingy, losing the confidence and self-esteem that would have enabled her to overcome adversity.

Two women of the lower classes who succeed on their level are contrasted with Lily. Gerty Farish, a social worker and close friend of Lily's, lives in a humble apartment in lower Manhattan. At first, Gerty is seen as dissatisfied with life. Her lonliness, her cramped surroundings, her inability to win Lawrence Seldon's affection—all weigh heavily on her and at times make her jealous of Lily, who seems to have all the things she has not. But when Lily falls from her position and relies on Gerty for moral support, Gerty reflects a moral courage and stability that makes her life, although dull, successful. Her sense of resignation and compassion for others enables her to overcome the adversities of life.

Identical traits are found in Nettie Crane, a consumptive shopgirl who once benefitted by a charitable donation from Lily to Gerty's self-help women's club. When Lily first meets Nettie, she considers her a thin and shabby figure, "one of the discouraged victims of overwork and anaemic parentage, one of the superfluous fragments of life destined to be swept prematurely into that social refuse heap. . . ." (p. 325) But when Lily again meets her, it is now Lily who is morally and economically destitute, while Nettie's "frail envelope" is "alive with hope and energy; whatever fate the future reserved for her, she would not be passed into the refuse heap without a struggle." (p. 325) More than resignation has enabled Nettie to survive, for she has found love with a husband and a child. It is this family bond that has provided her with the will to survive in the perilous world of New York City, and this resignation slowly dawns on Lily:

> The poor little working-girl who had found strength to gather up the fragments of her life and build herself a shelter with them seemed to Lily to have reached the central truth of existence. It was a meagre enough life, on the grim edge of poverty, with scant margin for possibilities of sickness or mischance, but it had the frail, audacious permanence of a bird's nest built on the edge of a cliff—a mere wisp of leaves and straw, yet so put together that the lives entrusted to it may hang safely over the abyss. (p. 332)

Unfortunately, Lily lacks these two traits. They would have enabled her to survive despite her adversity. But without the inbred resignation of a Gerty Farish or the love of a man like Nettie Crane's husband, Lily is doomed to an end of lonliness and death.

Lily's lonliness reflects the fundamental isolation of New York City life. In a deterministic universe, individuals are pitted against each other in their attempt to survive. When people begin to help each other, however, the power of such a universe begins to falter since the strength of the group compounds the strength of the individual against deterministic forces. Lily finds this strength when she seeks the solace and friendship of Gerty Farish and Nettie Crane, but towards the end of the novel she withdraws from everyone and everything—society, friends, and eventually life itself. Isolation, therefore, is a problem that Lily is unable to overcome, and for Edith Wharton it becomes the intrinsic problem of a large, impersonal city such as New York. Practically everyone in this novel is isolated to some degree.

Lily's isolation unfolds on three levels as the novel progresses. At first she is economically isolated from her friends and dissatisfied with her position as a mere "hanger-on." Although she attends their balls and summer parties, she is never able to completely enter into their lives as an equal. And when she takes up gambling at the Trenors, she loses herself in the nagging concern of her insolvency, and begins to recognize how completely isolated she is from her rich friends:

> A few years ago it had sufficed her: she had taken her daily meed of pleasure without caring who provided it. Now she was beginning to chafe at the obligations it imposed, to feel herself a mere pensioner on the splendour which had once seemed to belong to her. (p. 29)

Her economic isolation becomes complete when she is disinherited by her aunt who is horrified by Lily's "fast" life. For the first time Lily is utterly alone:

> No one looked at her, no one seemed aware of her presence; she was probing the very depths of insignificance. And under her sense of the collective indifference came the acuter pang of hopes deceived. (p. 231)

As the novel progresses, Lily's isolation becomes more ominous. Society rejects her when Bertha Dorset wrongfully accuses her of

41

adultery, and she, in turn, rejects all humanity and drifts away from even those who would like to help her.

While at first dependent on Gerty Farish for moral support, she later feels guilty for being a burden and seeks solace in her tiny room at the boardinghouse:

> Something of her mother's fierce shrinking from observation and sympathy was beginning to develop in her, and the promiscuity of small quarters and close intimacy seemed, on the whole, less endurable than the solitude of a hall bedroom in a house where she could come and go unremarked among other workers. (p. 297)

Later she refuses the proffered assistance of Simon Rosedale who wants to loan her some money to help overcome financial difficulties; she falls increasingly under the influence of a narcotic drug that dulls her sensations and memories; and finally, before she dies, she withdraws one evening to Bryant Park, spiritually isolated from the bustle of her fellow New Yorkers:

> That melancholy pleasure-ground was almost deserted when she entered it, and she sank down on an empty bench in the glare of an electric street-lamp. The warmth of the fire had passed out of her veins, and she told herself that she must not sit long in the penetrating dampness which struck up from the wet asphalt. But her willpower seemed to have spent itself in a last great effort, and she was lost in the blank reaction which follows on an unwonted expenditure of energy. (p. 323)

Lily's growing isolation, from economic to spiritual, mirrors again the deterministic City where each person is on his own, and where looking out for oneself is the principal preoccupation. Her growing depression is nurtured by this aspect of city life, and even the few hands that are held out to her in assistance are ignored by her as she increasingly falls under its numbing influence.

Lily's condition, however, is not unique, for she reflects a malaise that Wharton views as concomitant to city life. The gulf between the rich and the poor is so wide that neither class has any understanding or awareness of the other. As a representative of the wealthy, the Van Osburghs possess a "force of negation which eliminated everything beyond their own range of perception." (p. 52) This statement applies to everyone within Lily's higher social circle, and even she finds herself a stranger in their society. Judy

Trenor, supposedly one of Lily's closest friends, has virtually no understanding of Lily's pecuniary difficulties:

> Judy knew it must be "horrid" for poor Lily to have to stop to consider whether she could afford real lace on her petticoats, and not to have a motor car and a steam-yacht at her orders; but the daily friction of unpaid bills, the daily nibble of small temptations to expenditure, were trials as far out of her experience as the domestic problems of the charwoman. (p. 82)

The lower classes are as similarly ignorant of the rich who appear to them as an abstract vision of beauty and elegance. Consequently, Gerty's perception of Lily's environment is different from that held by Lily who is familiar with the glittering life: "Such flashes of joy as Lily moved in would have blinded Miss Farish, who was accustomed, in the way of happiness, to such scant light as shone through the cracks of other people's lives." (p. 158)

The ignorance and confusion that individuals and classes have for each other in *The House of Mirth* is further compounded by the overall rootlessness of city life. For Wharton, the City has no focus, no traditions strong enough to give it a sense of stability or permanence that would make it tangible or real. Lily's life in many ways reflects this instability and rootlessness, a fact she realizes toward the end of the novel:

> That was the feeling which possessed her now, the feeling of being something rootless and ephemeral, mere spindrift of the whirling surface of existence, without anything to which the poor little tentacles of self could cling before the awful flood submerged them. And as she looked back she saw that there had never been a time when she had had any real relation to life. Her parents too had been rootless, blown hither and thither on every wind of fashion, without any personal existence to shelter them from its shifting gusts. She herself had grown up without any one spot of earth being dearer to her than another; there was no centre of early pieties, of grave endearing traditions, to which her heart could revert and from which it could draw strength for itself and tenderness for others. (p. 331)

Behind this rootlessness and isolation of the characters in *The House of Mirth*, there lies a creeping paralysis that permeates every level of existence—social, economic, and moral—as it dehumanizes individuals and forces them into behavior patterns from which no deviation is possible without disasterous consequences. All of

Lily's rich friends are confined to a particular behavior of party-giving and superficial living:

> How dreary and trivial these people were! Lily reviewed them with a scornful impatience: Carry Fisher, with her shoulders, her eyes, her divorces, her general air of embodying a "spicy paragraph"; young Silverton, who had meant to live on proof-reading and write an epic, and who now lived on his friends and had become critical of truffles; Alice Wetherall, an animated visiting-list whose most fervid convictions turned on the wording of invitations and the engraving of dinner-cards; Wetherall, with his perpetual nervous nod of acquiescence, his air of agreeing with people before he knew what they were saying; Jack Stepney, with his confident smile and anxious eyes, half-way between the sheriff and an heiress; Gwen Van Osburgh, with all the guileless confidence of a young girl who has always been told that there is no one richer than her father. (p. 59)

Women in particular are dehumanized and trapped into this specific social behavior. Judy Trenor has completely lost her identity in a whirl of elegant party-giving. She exists "only as a hostess, not so much from any exaggerated instinct of hospitality as because she could not sustain life except in a crowd." (p. 44) Another friend, Mrs. Hatch, has lost her identity in the "torrid splendor" of elegant hotel living and, with the other ladies of her class, travels aimlessly "into vague metropolitan distances, whence they return, still more wane from the weight of their sables, to be sucked back into the stifling inertia of the hotel routine." (p. 283) Much of Lily's life is similarly trapped within a prison of social mores. She points out to Seldon how women are slaves to fashion and that while men can dress with an air of independence, no woman dares attempt liberties for "Who wants a dingy woman? We are expected to be pretty and well-dressed till we drop—and if we can't keep it up alone, we have to go into partnership." (p. 14) Similarly, the moral strictures of society mandate that marriageable women like Lily must scrupulously maintain an air of genteel propriety. Women are more susceptible to gossip than men and furthermore, as Lily points out to Gerty, the truth frequently does not figure in a woman's reputation: "What is truth? Where a woman is concerned, it's the story that's easiest to believe." (pp. 233-234)

On another level, Lily finds herself a prisoner within the male-dominated world of economics and law. She has to rely on Gus Trenor for stock market tips and ends up being compromised by his assistance. Later, in her attempt to circumvent the delays in her inheritance from her aunt, she finds herself confronting a legal system unsympathetic to women. Mrs. Peniston's lawyer is completely unmoved by Lily's pleas, and Lily leaves from a meeting with him with a sense of her "powerlessness of beauty and charm against the unfeeling processes of the law." (p. 238) No wonder then that in Seldon's imagination she appears manacled to a world that demands from her elegance and decorum on its own terms:

> As he watched her hand, polished as a bit of old ivory, with its slender pink nails and the sapphire bracelet slipping over her wrist, he was struck with the irony of suggesting to her such a life as his cousin Gertrude Farish had chosen. She was so evidently the victim of the civilization which had produced her that the links of her bracelet seemed like manacles chaining her to her fate. (p. 9)

The upper classes, however, are not the only ones imprisoned within their environment. The middle class and working poor find themselves also shackled, but to an entirely different form of existence. Wharton portrays them as people who have been bled white by their occupations. The office girls that Lily stands out amongst at Grand Central Station in Chapter One are "sallow-faced girls in preposterous hats and flat-chested women struggling with paper bundles and palm-leaf fans." (p. 7) Gerty Farish is similarly dull and unfashionable, wearing clothes of "useful" colors and "subdued lines." (p. 94) There are also the "batch of pale men on small salaries" who have "grown grey in the management of the Gryce estate. . . ." (pp. 25-26) At the milliner's establishment where Lily works, the girls have poor complexions as a result of the "unwholesomeness of hot air and sedentary toil. . . ." (p. 292) Their homes are as cramped as Gerty's apartment and have vistas as limited as Lily's flat that looks out on "sallow . . . brick walls and fire-escapes. . . ." (p. 256)

A moral paralysis accompanies the social paralysis in the novel as well. Relationships between men and women are largely perverse. Rosedale, like all the men of his economic standing, views Lily strictly as a desirable item that may enhance his chances for getting into high society. Gus Trenor values her as purchased entertainment and a support of his tired ego; Ned Van Alstyne fails to see beyond her purely physical sensuous appeal when she appears in a tableau dressed as a figure from a Reynolds painting: " 'Deuced bold thing to show herself in that get-up; but gad, there isn't a break in the lines anywhere, and I suppose she wanted us to know it!' " (p. 142)

A moral paralysis infects New York marriages. Extramarital affairs are commonplace, and Lily's reputation is sacrificed in order to satisfy the lusts of her friends. Her childhood recollection of her parents further points to this element of decay in society. Her mother was a selfish woman and her father's self-effacement and preoccupation with business altogether resulted in a marriage without love or tenderness:

> Ruling the turbulent element called home was the vigorous and determined figure of a mother still young enough to dance her ball-dresses to rags, while the hazy outline of a neutral-tinted father filled an intermediate space between the butler and the man who came to wind the clocks. Even to the eyes of infancy, Mrs. Hudson Bart had appeared young; but Lily could not recall the time when her father had not been bald and slightly stooping, with streaks of grey in his hair and a tired walk. It was a shock to her to learn afterward that he was but two years older than her mother. (pp. 32-33)

Lily recalls how her mother ceased to view her father as a functional part of the marriage after his bankruptcy, and how he died a heartbroken man. Lily has stronger feelings for her father, but even her sensations are greatly attenuated:

> She seemed always to have seen him through a blur—first of sleepiness, then of distance and indifference—and now the fog had thickened till he was almost indistinguishable. If she could have performed any little services for him or have exchanged with him a few of those affecting words which an extensive perusal of fiction had led her to connect with such occasions, the filial instinct might have stirred in her; but her pity, finding no active expression, remained in a state of spectatorship, overshadowed by her mother's grim, unflagging resentment. (pp. 36-37)

This perversion of sentiment is again witnessed in the degeneration of Mrs. Van Osburgh's motherly love into a preoccupation for placing her daughters and sons "one by one in enviable niches of existence through affluent marriages." (p. 96)

Moral paralysis extends from the family into every aspect of human relationship in *The House of Mirth*. Friendship is determined by the size of one's bank account or attendance at the "right" church. Consequently, Rosedale constitutes a dilemma for most of Lily's friends. As a Jew, he is viewed as a "novelty," an outsider "who had been served up and rejected at the social board a dozen times. . . ." (p. 19) But his increasing wealth precludes total rejection, and he soon gains a grudging admittance into select society.

Lawrence Seldon first appears in the novel as Lily's protector, and the person most capable of expanding her vision of life. In Chapter Six he confronts Lily with his philosophy of the "republic of the spirit," a concept of personal freedom "from everything— from money, from poverty, from care and anxiety, from all the material accidents." (pp. 72-73) Seldon gives Lily hope, but he himself fails to realize his own ideals; imprisoned and paralyzed by the standards of a society he rejects, he is powerless to rescue her from her fall during the latter half of the novel, and even accepts the standard view of her:

> It was much simpler for him to judge Miss Bart by her habitual conduct than by the rare deviations from it which had thrown her so disturbingly in his way; and every act of hers which made the recurrence of such deviations more unlikely confirmed the sense of relief with which he returned to the conventional view of her. (p. 281)

Lily's strongest inspiration, indeed, comes from Nettie Crane. The girl has an inner strength that Lily grows to admire, and this strength offers for Lily a vision of stability in a chaotic world, a stability that is tenuous yet permanent. Unfortunately for Lily, this awareness comes too late.

As might be expected, the contemporary critical reaction to Wharton's view of New York society was less than complimentary. Although the book was a bestseller, critics reacted with anger and disgust to the "vulgar, heartless, uninteresting, or immoral" characters presented.[7] What they failed to realize was that Wharton was writing about New York society as she perceived it. The influences acting on her heroine were in many ways identical to those she herself had experienced as a young socialite. Having grown up in the city and married into wealth, she knew the pitfalls of high society and especially those found in New York City. The men in her family indulged in sea-fishing, boat racing, and hunting. The women oversaw elaborate dinner parties. Although she later referred in her autobiography to this society as having always displayed the highest standards in education and good manners, one can easily detect a sense of alienation in *The House of Mirth*. Like Lily, she had lost her father at an early age, and her family, while never poor, was reduced to a brownstone sobriety similar to that of Lily's Aunt Peniston. Within this enclave of conservative tastes she looked out with a jaunticed eye on the post-Civil War millionaires, the "lords of Pittsburgh," as she referred to them, the "invaders" of an older and simpler New York society who brought into it the corrupting influence and arrogant display of wealth.

Further parallels can be drawn with other characters. Percy Gryce, the awkward, hopelessly tied-to-his-mother's-apron-strings youth, whom Lily almost seduces, bears a resemblance to a Harry Stevens to whom Edith was briefly engaged during the summer of 1883 when she was nineteen. His mother, a pompous, domineering socialite who partied with the Vanderbilts, had previously married one of her children into European nobility and did not look kindly on a possible match between her son and Edith. It was soon broken. Another parallel can be drawn between Lawrence Seldon and Edith's life-long lawyer friend, Walter Berry, whom she met in 1884 and who frequently advised and edited her writings.

Finally, the gossip that surrounds Lily plagued Edith Wharton during her turbulent marriage to Teddy, thirteen years her senior, a handsome, easy-going sportsman, clubman, and philanderer. From the beginning he displayed little interest in Edith's literary or artistic activities. Their incompatibility, further compounded by their childless marriage, Teddy's frequent infidelities and mental breakdowns, resulted in divorce in 1913, a deed for which his side of the family never forgave her. At the time of her divorce, Wharton's alienation was so complete she hardly felt her suffering because she had willed herself to live apart from it in the world of her own creation—her writing. Consequently, like Lily, she too had come to realize the limitations of luxury and the unsatisfied hopelessness of an elegant home if it lacks love and understanding.

Apart from the glittering world of the upper Fifth Avenue mansions in *The House of Mirth* are the slums in Stephen Crane's *Maggie: A Girl of the Streets*. Crane's novelette is a powerful expose of slum life that further compliments our image of New York City at the turn of the century.

For Crane, slum life can be as illusionary as the life of the rich. On the surface there can appear a tawdry glitter that amuses and beguiles while masking a seething inner ugliness. The saloons Crane depicts reflect this dual character. Maggie's lover, Pete, works in such a place, a dive that has aristocratic pretensions boasting "imitation leather" wallpaper, a "shining bar of counterfeit massiveness," and "pyramids of shimmering glasses that were never disturbed" and multiplied by mirrors set in the face of the sideboard. Overall, the saloon presents an ambiance of "opulence and geometrical accuracy," but this is only an illusion, in sharp contrast with the asymmetrical disorder, chaos, and grimness of the world outside its doors.[8] This world is far more evident in the entertainment halls Pete and Maggie frequent. At one, the:

> orchestra of yellow silk women and bald-headed men gave vent to a few bars of anticipatory music and a girl, in a pink dress with short skirts, galloped upon the stage. She smiled upon the throng as if in acknowledgment of a warm welcome, and began to walk to and fro, making profuse gesticulations and singing, in brazen soprano tones, a song, the words of which were inaudible. When she broke into the swift rattling measures of a chorus some half tipsy men near the stage joined in the rollicking refrain and glasses were pounded rhythmically upon the tables. (p. 28)

Later they frequent a "hall of irregular shape" where a

> submissive orchestra dictated to by a spectacled man with frowsy hair and a dress suit, industriously followed the bobs of his head and the waves of his baton. A ballad singer, in a dress of flaming scarlet, sang in the inevitable voice of brass. When she vanished, men seated at the tables near the front applauded loudly, pounding the polished wood with their beer glasses. She returned attired in less gown, and sang again. She received another enthusiastic encore. (p. 48)

Their final haunt is a "hilarious hall" with "twenty-eight tables and twenty-eight women and a crowd of smoking men."

> Valiant noise was made on a stage at the end of the hall by an orchestra composed of men who looked as if they had just happened in. Soiled waiters ran to and fro, swooping down like hawks on the unwary in the throng; clattering along the aisles with trays covered with glasses; stumbling over women's skirts and charging

> two prices for everything but beer, all with a swiftness that blurred
> the view of the cocoanut palms and dusty monstrosities painted
> upon the walls of the room. (p. 54)

Each club represents to a greater degree a tawdry, frenetic quality of city life—and especially the Bowery. Under the facades of respectability and elegance lie the seedier truths that Crane encountered on the lower East Side, and it is these truths he confronts directly in his novelette.

Like Edith Wharton, Crane views the City as a dehumanizing environment, a place where the inhabitants lose their human identity and assume the City's personality. In the slums the brutality and coarseness of everyday life destroys every vestige of humanity. The tenement where Maggie's family lives epitomizes this quality. It is described as a "dark region" where "a dozen gruesome doorways gave up loads of babies to the street and the gutter." Mankind is reduced to substance without reason, intellect, or even soul. In the slums, such values do not exist. Only the physical, the apparent, are acknowledged:

> A wind of early autumn raised yellow dust from cobbles and
> swirled it against an hundred windows. Long streamers of gar-
> ments fluttered from fire-escapes. In all unhandy places there were
> buckets, brooms, rags and bottles. In the street infants played or
> fought with other infants or sat stupidly in the way of vehicles.
> Formidable women, with uncombed hair and disordered dress, gos-
> siped while leaning on railings, or screamed in frantic quarrels.
> Withered persons, in curious postures of submission to something,
> sat smoking pipes in obscure corners. A thousand odors of cooking
> food came forth to the street. The building quivered and creaked
> from the weight of humanity stamping about in its bowels. (p. 7)

The inhabitants of these tenement houses become faceless, nameless entities in Crane's novel. He wishes to emphasize the impersonal atmosphere of the City, and its inhabitants are concomitantly stripped of all but their physical presence.

In the slums humanity is replaced with brute drives for survival. Thus, Maggie's brother first appears in the novel as a nameless little boy standing upon a heap of gravel "for the honor of Rum alley" with the face of a "tiny, insane demon" as he defends his turf against an invading gang from Devil's row. (p. 3) In a drunken slumber Maggie's mother is similarly presented in strictly physical terms with an enlarged face, yellow brows, and "shaded eyelids that had grown blue." "Her bare, red arms were thrown out above her head in positions of exhaustion, something, mayhap, like those of a sated villain." (p. 14) During the day she wanders the streets, a nameless alcoholic, thrown out of saloons and tormented by local children. Her grey hair becomes "knotted masses about her shoulders," her face "crimsomed and wet with perspiration," her eyes, "a rolling glare." (p. 35) Hattie, Jimmy's girl, appears as a "forlorn woman" amidst a crowd of people "desperately bound on missions" with thoughts "fixed on distant dinners." (p. 59) And by the end of the story Maggie herself becomes another faceless prostitute, wandering the streets of nameless men and women, one of the painted ladies of the City, "changing glances at men who passed her, giving smiling invitations to men of rural or untaught pattern and usually seeming sedately unconscious of the men with a metropolitan seal upon their faces." (p. 66)

In Crane's novel each character exists in an existentialist universe, deriving his or her identity from the local surroundings. A beggar woman in Chapter Three blends in with the stones of Fifth Avenue, dehumanized to such a point that she appears "immovable and hideous, like an idol" (p. 12); a saloon hall dancer in Chapter Seven presents a "smile of stereotyped enthusiasm" and later falls into "grotesque attitudes which were at the time popular among the dancers" (p. 29); Maggie's fellow workers at the collar and cuff establishment appear to her like "mere mechanical contrivances sewing seams and grinding out, with heads bended over their work, tales of imagined or real girl-hood happiness, past drunks, the baby at home, and unpaid wages." (p. 31) The City surrounding these characters serves as a backdrop of decayed values, stripping the working class of its identity and depriving it of the various traits that would make it human. People become victims, powerless against the fate offered by the City.

In the slums, life has become so tainted by the primeaval conflict for survival that the old cliches about the purity and inno cence of childhood are no longer valid. The battle between Jimmy and the Devil's Row kids is not only graphic in its depiction, it is also disturbing in its allusions. The children degenerate into savages who "leer gloatingly" over the battered and bloody face of a beaten child. (p. 4)

The fight also reflects Crane's theme that life is a war on all levels within the slums. Jimmy is a personification of this theme.

As an adolescent he becomes hardened, "a young man of leather," who is continually at odds with his environment:

> During that time his sneer became chronic. He studied human nature in the gutter, and found it no worse than he thought he had reason to believe it. He never conceived a respect for the world, because he had begun with no idols. . . . (p. 16)

He hates well-dressed men who to him are weak since "all good coats covered faint hearts." He despises the conventional middle-class with its "obvious Christians and ciphers with the chrysanthemums of aristocracy in their button-holes." As a trucker he sits aloft the driver's seat scornfully wrathful and contemptuous of the humanity around him:

> He became so sharp that he believed in nothing. To him the police were always actuated by malignant impulses and the rest of the world was composed, for the most part, of despicable creatures who were all trying to take advantage of him and with whom, in defense, he was obliged to quarrel on all possible occasions. He himself occupied a down-trodden position that had a private but distinct element of grandeur in its isolation. (pp. 17-18)

The only thing Jimmy can believe in is brute force. The slums have deprived him of the finer sensibilities, and he sinks lower and lower in this deterministic jungle.

In this, he is similar to Pete, Maggie's lover, who also has an admiration for brute force and a scorn for all things intellectual and peaceful. While visiting the zoo with Maggie, Pete applauds a very small monkey who threatens to "thrash a cageful because one of them had pulled his tail. . . ." (p. 33) In Chapter Eleven he, Jimmie and a friend test their brute courage in a fight that is graphic in its blood-letting imagery:

> Each head was huddled between its owner's shoulders, and arms were swinging with marvelous rapidity. Feet scraped to and fro with a loud scratching sound upon the sanded floor. Blows left crimson blotches upon pale skin. The curses of the first quarter minute of the fight died away. The breaths of the fighters came wheezingly from their lips and the three chests were straining and heaving. Pete at intervals gave vent to low, labored hisses, that

sounded like a desire to kill. Jimmie's ally gibbered at times like a wounded maniac, Jimmie was silent, fighting with the face of a sacrificial priest. The rage of fear shone in all their eyes and their blood-colored fists swirled. (pp. 46-47)

Not until Hemingway would a fight be described in similar realistic tones.

Besides brute strength, survival is determined by selfishness and cunning. The tenement dwellers, secure behind their doors and impervious to the sufferings of others except when it offers a transient form of entertainment, enjoy listening to the fighting between Maggie's parents. In the City, one is never alone in the physical sense. There are the prying eyes of the neighbors when Maggie returns disgraced to her family in Chapter Fifteen, but a distance is always maintained and no one reaches out to help her. True communication is never established.

Through the open doors curious eyes stared in at Maggie. Children ventured into the room and ogled her, as if they formed the front row at a theatre. Women, without, bended toward each other and whispered, nodding their heads with airs of profound philosophy. (p. 61)

Later, in a similar vein, the neighbors gather to witness Mrs. Johnson's tears for her dead daughter, staring at her "as if watching the contortions of a dying dog." (p. 73)

Cunning selfishness is the principal trait of Jimmie who invites a reluctant friend to help him thrash Pete, but later abandons him and escapes through a side entrance when the police arrive to break up the disturbance. From a dark, safe corner he sees the policemen march his friend and Pete off to the local station house. At first Jimmie thinks of rescuing his friend, but shrugs it off with a phrase frequently repeated by other characters in the novel: "Ah, what deh hell?" (p. 48)

The relationship between men and women further demonstrates this deterministic influence of the City. In men's eyes, women are little more than sex objects, devoid of humanity. They are to be used and abused but not loved. Maggie slowly becomes aware of this as the novel progresses. In Chapter Five she is described as having blossomed in a mud puddle, and grown to be "a most rare and wonderful production of a tenement district, a pretty girl." (p. 20) But in the dance halls her physical beauty is perverted by the lecherous stares of the "Grey-headed men, wonderfully pathetic in their dissipation," and the "smooth cheeked boys, some of them with faces of stone and mouths of sin, not nearly so pathetic as the grey heads. . . ." (p. 50) In this world all women are equated as objects.

Hattie, who has been psychologically brutalized and abandoned by Jimmie, continues to follow him around, a "forlorn woman dodging about like a scout." (p. 60) Jimmie feels no remorse for his abusive treatment of her. Nor, similarly, does Pete feel any remorse when he abandons Maggie:

> Pete did not consider that he had ruined Maggie. If he had thought that her soul could never smile again, he would have believed the mother and brother, who were pyrotechnic over the affair, to be responsible for it. (p. 62)

Ironically, like all the people in the tenement house, Jimmie is too ego-oriented to contemplate the parallel between his behavior to Hattie and Pete's abuse of Maggie. As a result, he damns his sister and rejects her when she comes to him for help.

Also contributing to the City's determinism is the general sense of isolation that surrounds all the characters in the novel. While the City's environment precludes physical isolation, characters remain emotionally isolated from each other. There is no room for understanding, sympathy, or kindness in Crane's City, and it is this that makes the streets particularly mean.

Crane brilliantly portrays this paradoxical quality of city life in the first chapter. The observers of the fight between Jimmie and the Devil's Row gang view it at a distance. They are a part of the action but do not become involved with it:

> From a window of an apartment house that upreared its form from amid squat, ignorant stables, there leaned a curious woman. Some laborers, unloading a scow at a dock at the river, paused for a moment and regarded the fight. The engineer of a passive tugboat hung lazily to a railing and watched. Over on the Island, a worm of yellow convicts came from the shadow of a grey ominous building and crawled slowly along the river's bank. (p. 4)

The convicts stand out as the dominant symbol in this passage, for like the people on the shore, they are a part of the action and yet separate from it. Each individual, like the convicts, is shackled to his particular position. Laborers are unloading at the dock, a woman leans from an apartment building, an engineer rests on a railing of a tugboat—each character is confined and isolated, yet the City creates, because of its compactness, an illusion of togetherness.

None of the characters in *Maggie* effectively communicates with any other. Jimmie, for example, is very much a part of the city scene. He enjoys standing on street corners dreaming "blood red dreams" when pretty women pass by; he enjoys menacing mankind and feels as though he is merging into the center of things: "On the corners he was in life and of life. The world was going on and he was there to perceive it." (p. 16) But his perception, however Whitmanesque in tone, never achieves an element of sympathy that would allow him to understand mankind. Instead, we find him as a truckdriver damning and cursing everything and everyone around him and especially the police who frequently "climb up, drag him from his perch and beat him." (p. 17) He admires the fire engines, for they are the ultimate symbol of isolation—shiny and bright, whizzing through the streets, pulled by demonic horses at breakneck speed, impervious to everything around them. Jimmie is especially in awe of their reputation for overturning street cars: "Those leaping horses, striking sparks from the cobbles in their forward lunge, were creatures to be ineffably admired. The clang of the gong pierced his breast like a noise of remembered war." (p. 19) Only one character makes an effort to overcome the inherent isolation around her—Maggie. But she is alone in her attempt, and her efforts end in failure, brutalized by her mother and scorned by her brother and her lover.

Rejected by her family, her other attempts to communicate are pathetic. She accosts a clergyman, "a stout gentlemen in a silk hat and a chaste black coat, whose decorous row of buttons reached from his chin to his knees." But despite his benevolent appearance, his heart is cold to her plea, and he saves his "respectability" with a vigorous sidestep. "He did not wish to save a soul. For how was he to know that there was a soul before him that needed saving." (p. 65) As a prostitute, she sinks to greater depths of isolation. In Chapter Seventeen she is spurned by a tall young man in evening dress, a stout gentleman "with pompous and philanthropic whiskers," a man in business clothes, a laboring man, and finally a drunk. She is rejected by all she meets until at the end of the story, alongside the polluted river and amongst hidden factories, she meets a man who wants her services. He is a figure who personifies the moral degeneration of the City that has destroyed Maggie:

> On going forward she perceived it to be a huge fat man in torn and greasy garments. His grey hair straggled down over his forehead. His small, bleared eyes, sparkling from amidst great rolls of red fat, swept eagerly over the girl's upturned face. He laughed, his brown, disordered teeth gleaming under a grey, grizzled moustache from which beer-drops dripped. His whole body gently quivered and shook like that of a dead jelly fish. Chuckling and leering, he followed the girl of the crimson legions. (p. 68)

This motif of despair and isolation concludes with Maggie's death set against the distant sounds of joyful merrymakers of "seeming unapproachableness." (p. 68)

Maggie's deterministic end, however, is not entirely free of a self-destructive will. In a letter to Miss Catherine Harris in 1896, Crane noted that the "route of Bowery life is a sort of cowardice. Perhaps I mean a lack of ambition or to willingly be knocked flat and accept the licking." (p. 2) In light of this observation, Crane intended his characters as part victims as well as victimizers who, through their own ignorance or stupidity, perpetuated their own destructive environment. Pete and Jimmie best exemplify this characteristic, since both are excessively wrapped up in aggrandized macho self-images that make them insensitive to the environment around them and incapable of conceiving moral principles. Their sense of power is not true strength but instead a deeply rooted vanity.

Maggie's dilemma begins with her inability to comprehend this trait in Pete's personality. To her, he appears to be heroic:

> His mannerisms stamped him as a man who had a correct sense of his personal superiority. There was valor and contempt for circumstances in the glance of his eye. He waved his hands like a man of the world, who dismisses religion and philosophy, and says "Fudge." He had certainly seen everything and with each curl of his lip, he declared that it amounted to nothing. Maggie thought he must be a very elegant and graceful bartender. (p. 21)

Maggie's inherently limited perspective prevents her from appreciating a different type of person. It is this perspective that taints every aspect of her life, and subverts every opportunity for moral guidance.

Furthermore, it is a perspective that has been reinforced in her home life. The principal form of communication in her family is violence. Her mother has brutalized her, and sibling quarrels frequently come to blows. Even dinner-time is reduced to a ritual of survival:

> The children scrambled hastily. With prodigious clatter they arranged themselves at table. The babe sat with his feet dangling high from a precarious infant chair and gorged his small stomach. Jimmie forced, with feverish rapidity, the grease-enveloped pieces between his wounded lips. Maggie, with side glances of fear of interruption, ate like a small pursued tigress. (pp. 10-11)

Other bad examples are found in the middle-and upper-class institutions that promulgate false ethics. Crane repeatedly condemns these institutions, such as the established churches of the day. In Chapter Four a preacher at a mission church dispenses his tainted charity with scorn:

> While they got warm at the stove, he told his hearers just where he calculated they stood with the Lord. Many of the sinners were impatient over the pictured depths of their degradation. They were waiting for soup-tickets.
>
> A reader of words of wind-demons might have been able to see the portions of a dialogue pass to and fro between the exhorter and his hearers.
>
> "You are damned," said the preacher. And the reader of sounds might have seen the reply go forth from the ragged people: "Where's our soup?" (p. 16)

Mrs. Johnson frequently revels in a maudlin, cliche-ridden imitation of contemporary ethics when she laments the "moral decay" of Maggie. Her astonishing inability to search her own soul makes her lamentations particularly ironic:

> She had never considered Maggie as a pearl dropped unstained into Rum Alley from Heaven, but she could not conceive how it was possible for her daughter to fall so low as to bring disgrace upon her family. She was terrific in denunciation of the girl's wickedness. (p. 51)

At the time of Maggie's death, Crane fittingly describes the mother at a table "eating like a fat monk in a picture." (p. 72) Her greed and selfishness are again caricatured against a backdrop of conventional morality.

Maggie's lover, Pete, is also described against a backdrop of conventional false ethics. After his cruel rejection of Maggie, we encounter him at a seedy saloon surrounded by prostitutes, beaming a pseudo-benevolence, "in the proper mode of missionaries." (p. 69) If Maggie is a Christ-like figure, suffering for the sins of those around her and more sinned against than sinning, Pete is an anti-Christ whose last appearance at the saloon becomes a perverted rendition of the Last Supper. Abandoned by his "disciples," the prostitutes, and described as an "offering priest," we see him alone in the bar cubicle in a perverse eucharistic tableau:

> The smoke from the lamps settled heavily down in the little compartment, obscuring the way out. The smell of oil, stifling in its intensity, pervaded the air. The wine from an overturned glass dripped softly down upon the blotches of the man's neck. (p. 72)

The gossipy old women in the Johnson's tenement also echo the pious platitudes of convention. They viciously gossip when Maggie is rejected by Pete, and finally join with Maggie's mother in an orgy of ritualistic mourning over the dead girl:

> The neighbors began to gather in the hall, staring in at the weeping woman. . . . A dozen women entered and lamented with her. Under their busy hands the rooms took on that appalling appearance of neatness and order with which death is greeted.
>
> Suddenly the door opened and a woman in a black gown rushed in with outstretched arms. "Ah, poor Mary," she cried, and tenderly embraced the moaning one.
>
> "Ah, what ter'ble affliction is dis," continued she. Her vocabulary was derived from mission churches. "Me poor Mary, how I feel fer yehs! Ah, what a ter'ble affliction is a disobed'ent chil'. (p. 73)

Another institution that Crane condemns is the theatre. Middle-class melodrama has filtered down to the lower classes of Maggie's world. Rather than present a higher set of values, it applauds the false ethics of convention and the status quo, offering no plan for reforming the evils of society. In Chapter Eight, Maggie gets caught up in the sentiments of such a show, rejoicing "at the way in which the poor and virtuous eventually surmounted the wealthy and wicked." (p. 35) The theatre fills her with false hope and a false sense of reality. It reinforces her tendency to incorrectly interpret the world and the people around her, and leaves her confused by the obvious inconsistencies of her life. There is no way she can effectively rise above her environment.

The dichotomy of Maggie's world was equally praised and condemned by the critics. For many, the ugly scenes of violence and degradation were, as the *New York Press* noted, not "clandestinely attractive." Many scenes were rejected for not being "wholly acceptable in literature."[9] Another critic complained that "its shadows are too deep and its lights too faint and evasive, missing, indeed, the highest aim of literature, which is to give some small degree of pleasure, at least, to the world, and to prove itself not a clog, but an aspiration in the uplifting of humanities heart."[10] Far-sighted critics praised *Maggie's* realistic scenes and Crane as a "master of slum slang."[11] And the "dean" of American letters, William D. Howells, even applauded its vivid portrait of lower New York slum life as well as its having the "quality of fatal necessity which dominates Greek tragedy."[12] But despite the efforts of Howells and others similarly minded, booksellers refused to sell *Maggie*.

The American reading public was not ready for the type of realism Crane presented—a realism that questioned American values and the greatest of American cities. Here were certainly no "pink valentines," as Crane scornfully referred to the saccarine literature of his day. Here instead, as Hamlin Garland, his close friend, noted, was a "voice of the slums" that reached out and confronted the reader with disquieting truths.[13] What startled the public was that the "truths" reflected a disillusionment and despair for America that rejected the conventional optimism of the times. In an age of rapid Western expansion and industrial growth, Crane's vision seemed almost sacrilegious.

But Crane knew better. His whole life reflected the City's tempo. As a preacher's son and later as the son of a widowed woman looking for ways to raise her family, Crane spent much of his youth on the move. Furthermore, he attended a number of colleges and never had a strong sense of home. In 1891 his home was the Bowery, for him "the most interesting place in New York."[14] In the next few years he would spend most of his time wandering through its streets, associating with every quality of human existence, carefully noting in detail mannerisms and language while staving off starvation writing stringers for local papers and living in "virtual madhouse dormitories of medical students and artists."[15]

As a journalist, he became involved with his world on the lower East Side of the City and reported it passionately. But he also adhered to the truth. "To keep close to this honesty is my supreme ambition," he wrote to a friend, and this is the principal factor behind the detailed imagery in *Maggie*.[16] Truth demands only two prerequisites, research and realism, and Crane found both in abundance in his City. He did not need the literary inspiration of a Howells or a Garland to point him in the right direction. The City was enough. Unlike his fellow writers, he did not hide the more unpleasant aspects of the City from the reader's eye. Barroom brawls, alcoholism, and suicide are his domain. After Crane's death in 1899, Howells aptly noted: "New York was essentially his inspiration, the New York of suffering and baffled and beaten life, of inarticulate or blasphemous life; and away from it he was not at home, with any theme, or any sort of character."[17]

Chapter Two

[1]Lloyd Morris, *Incredible New York* (New York: Random House, 1951), p. 241.

[2]*Ibid.*, p. 242.

[3]Bernard A. Weisberger, *Reaching For Empire* (New York: Time Inc., 1964), VIII, 74.

[4]*Ibid.*

[5]Morris, p. 233.

[6]Edith Wharton, *The House of Mirth* (1905; rpt. New York: New American Library, 1964), p. 7; henceforth all future references to this book will be followed with the page number(s).

[7]Grace Kellogg, *The Two Lives of Edith Wharton* (New York: Appleton Century, 1965), p. 110.

[8]Stephen Crane, "Maggie: A Girl of the Streets," in *The Portable Stephen Crane*, ed. Joseph Katz (New York: Viking Press, 1969), p. 43; henceforth all future references to this book will be followed with the page number(s).

[9]R.W. Stallman, *Stephen Crane: A Biography* (New York: George Bruziller, 1968), pp. 72-73.

[10]*Ibid.*, p. 51.

[11]p. 42.

[12]p. 47.

[13]p. 38.

[14]Edwin Cady, *Stephen Crane* (Boston: Twayne, 1980), p. 40.

[15]*Ibid.*, p. 41.

[16]p. 81.

[17]Stallman, p. 62.

CHAPTER III

The Dynamic City:
John Dos Passos' *Manhattan Transfer*

Two traits predominated in New York City during the years immediately following the conclusion of World War I: physical growth and spiritual change. Skyscrapers began to dominate the lower and midtown regions as more and more companies moved or founded their headquarters in Manhattan. A similar growth appeared in City services as the police and fire departments expanded and modernized their operations. New roads were built as well as an extensive mass transit system that interconnected the separate Boroughs. More movie houses and theaters appeared as Broadway, Times Square, and 42nd Street became the bywords for the cinemagraphic fantasies of Hollywood. But most significant was the rapid growth of the middle class whose members were composed of the sons and daughters of immigrants who came to the City at the turn of the century. Unlike their parents, they considered the American way of life not as a gift but as a right, and they set out to achieve that right working in the offices of midtown Manhattan by day and commuting by night to one of the apartment complexes that began to dominate the once rolling farmlands of Queens and the Bronx.

A restless class, it was unsatisfied with the ideals and mores of previous generations. From its ranks arose a new type of woman who considered herself totally liberated from the economic and social restrictions imposed upon her mother. She held jobs, wore shorter skirts, and bobbed her hair. Others within the class rebelled against the past by openly flaunting the laws of the land. Prohibition was ignored and the rapid growth of organized crime and political corruption were viewed with little concern. Finally, there arose a new generation of writers, many of them idealists but tainted with a touch of cynicism regarding their times. They had become disillusioned by the atrocities of World War I, and the unrestrained hedonism of the times further supported their belief that there was something seriously unsound at America's core. A number of writers joined radical causes and incorporated their beliefs in their writings. Dos Passos was among this group, and his novel, *Manhattan Transfer*, presents the clearest and most concise statement of a troubled yet dynamic post-War New York City.

Probably more than any other city in the Nation at the time, New York mirrored the boundless economic optimism of a prosperous post-War America. For many, New York was the most cosmopolitan city in the Nation, the most diverse in social and cultural customs, and, as such, the most international. As American businesses expanded their operations, they automatically established their headquarters in New York City. The City set the pace for great international business dealings and, due to Wall Street, kept the monetary pulsebeat of the Nation. Even architecture reflected this tempo, and fittingly the old Madison Square Presbyterian Church gave way to a fifty-story insurance building.

The Lincoln Building, the Chanin Building, and the Chrysler Tower were already dominating the midtown skyline, while farther North the majestic Sherry-Netherland, Savoy-Plaza, and the Pierre vied for attention among the new towering apartment buildings near Central Park. The new architecture changed the skyline, creating concrete valleys of darkness during the day, and a dazzling display of lights at night. It soon became the symbol of twentieth-century success. "Height is the new destination of American architecture," a British journalist noted in the 1920's: "Even in the distant suburbs of Manhattan . . . the twelve-floor building is there and the cottage is not."[1]

As the new skyscrapers changed the geometrical pattern of the skyline, they also imparted to the City a personality, an image, which no two observers viewed identically. The French novelist, Pierre Loti, found the skyscrapers unpleasant "gaunt giants" that "stretched their necks inordinately to see better" as they rose "higher and higher, terrifying and unbelievable."[2] The Russian novelist, Maxim Gorky, viewed them even harsher through Marxist eyes as "dull, heavy piles," of capitalistic greed filled with the "cold and haughty presumption" of a "glutton suffering from over-corpulency."[3] But others, conversely, found the City's new landscape fascinating. Charles Huard, another Frenchman, admired the "limitless silhouette" of the City and the dynamic urban vistas it presented.[4] Similarly, a German dramatist, Ludwig Fulda, praised the towering canyons as "not only colossal but beautiful."[5]

Visitors to the City also marvelled at how rapidly city services had improved. Everywhere a tourist turned, he confronted loud construction crews, and their work seemed interminable. As soon as roads were completed, they became jammed with automobiles testifying further to the need for still more highways. Was there no end in sight, mused one English traveller while caught on Broadway during the rush hour: "You could almost jump from roof to roof across the road."[6] A German count reported that there were more automobiles in New York City than in all of Europe; an Italian commentator devoted an entire chapter on the automobile when describing New York City in a book.

Of course, the increasing number of cars on city roads taxed other city services as well. A modernized police department bought motorcycles and squad cars and installed street-side telephones. If an accident occurred, it had to be dealt with speedily, before a serious traffic jam occurred. Concomitantly, the fire department expanded and modernized its operation. Gone were the days of the horse-drawn fire engines. Motorized fire trucks pushed through the congested city streets with such an uproar that many an uninitiated visitor to the City was startled at the commotion. "Nowhere do firemen rush to and fro so much as here," wrote a French visitor. "Every few yards there is a fire alarm or a fire hydrant as big as a siege-gun. The firemen arrive on the scene of the outbreak forty seconds after the alarm. Everything stops at the first piercing wail of their sirens, and the accompanying clang of bells, and the engines, beautiful as fire itself, go past with the swiftness of flames."[7] Not everyone viewed the increasing mechanization of the City with pleasure, however. Some, like H.G. Wells, found New York fast becoming a "steel-souled machine room," a city where "individuals count for nothing . . . the distinctive effect is the mass . . . the unprecedented multitudinousness of the thing."[8] By the late 1920's, an extensive network of underground and elevated trains extended outwards from Manhattan, linked to the suburban communities of Queens and the Bronx.

Such expansion had a profound effect on the size and distribution of the City's population. In 1910, nearly half of the City's inhabitants were concentrated on Manhattan Island. But by 1930,

Manhattan contained less than one-fifth of the City's seven million people. Brooklyn had two-and-one-half million, Queens more than one million, and the Bronx one-and-one-quarter million. The outer Boroughs were largely residential, as apartments pushed aside the sprawling farm communities of the previous century. Manhattan was dominated by office buildings. The City was taking on the image of a modern American city with its commercial center and outlying bedroom communities.

The increase in the City's population was only partly due to new immigration during the post-War years. The bulk of it reflected instead a second generation of New Yorkers—the sons and daughters of those who had come to the City in the 1890's. The new generation, better educated and trained to compete in the business world of lower and mid-town Manhattan, wanted a better life than that of their parents. The once rural communities of Sunnyside, Forest Hills, and Kew Gardens were now the homes for a rising middle class of office workers. In Brooklyn, snug, small houses went up alongside apartment complexes. The simplicity and orderliness of these communities reflected the people living in them. They possessed the basic refinements of a new age—a colored tile bath, an electric kitchenette, a studio couch, chromium-plated chairs, a folding table, and always a record-player or a radio. Newness was the dominant trait.

The middle class greatly influenced the temperament of the City. Unlike the rich and poor classes of the polarized City at the turn of the century, the middle class was not carefully defined or restricted by set rules or borders. They had evolved from the ranks of the poor but freely speculated with the rich on a runaway bull market that promised limitless prosperity. Buying stock on margin was the thing of the day, and numerous stories circulated on how a nominal investment could reap huge returns. Clerks, taxi drivers, shopkeepers, schoolteachers, and housewives dreamed of quick riches and of the sudden prosperity of those who were lucky enough to get the right "tips."

Change, therefore, became the prominent feature of the City under the middle class of the 1920's. As a class, they were always on the move—not only commuting between job and home, but from job to job, apartment to apartment. As a result, communities became highly unstable and rapidly lost their individuality. Movement was considered the sign of success, for no one upwardly mobile was expected to stay in any one place for too long. The City became restless and experimental, even daring, in its approach to life. For many, the City became a symbol of the new America. A British journalist visiting in 1928 sensed this vitality and noted how New York was a place for "standardizing ideas," in that it was the first to set the tone for the Nation and even the world: "The very thought of Broadway, the Main Street of all America, thrills millions who are scattered far and wide."[9]

But for others the frenetic instability foretold serious problems too. Paul Morand, the French novelist, envisioned the City's vitality as inherently violent—not criminally violent but haphazardly disoriented in objectives: "People are always moving," he complained. "The only permanent addresses are those of banks. People change jobs as they change houses. The town is no less changing. One builds for thirty years; those buildings have no past and no future either. Some districts alter their appearance in one season . . . Everything goes fast . . . New York is a perpetual thunderstorm."[10]

Part of the thunderstorm involved the City's social structure. The poor were no longer derived from the immigrant stock that had flocked to America in earlier years. Those that had made it were now out of the ghettoes leaving behind a more entrenched type of poverty for which there was no quick remedy. The millionaires of the 1920's were similarly different from the rich at the turn of the century. They lived far less isolated, secluded lives. Gone were the uptown mansions of the Vanderbilts and Astors, now replaced by luxury apartment dwellings with terraced penthouses. Nor did the rich live exclusively on upper Fifth Avenue; Park Avenue and Sutton Place became the new addresses for many millionaires. Fashionable apartments could easily demand rents as high as four thousand dollars a month, but on the outside they resembled more modest, middle-class dwellings. The *noveau riche* sported an element of *declasse* which for some observers reflected "restraint and good taste."[11] The wealthy, while still exerting an influence on the social life of the City, became more invisible. The "great social names," as Ford Maddox Ford observed, had disappeared: "There is a very gay, insouciant, and enormously expensive social life in New York, but relatively few names swim to the surface of its whirlpool and those that do are forever changing."[12]

New York's intellectual community also presented changing ideas and attitudes. Traditional views of America and American business came under attack by radical thinkers who frequented the cafes of Greenwich Village. Disillusioned by World War I and its use of modern, highly destructive technology, many questioned the values of contemporary American and European society. They blamed the War on the special business interests and, unlike the average American who applauded the booming times, found themselves confused and alienated by a world they saw as inherently false and cruel.

Others were further disillusioned by the execution of Sacco and Vanzetti. Nicola Sacco and Bartolomeo Vanzetti, two anarchists and draft-dodgers, were arrested on May 5, 1920, and charged with participation in a payroll robbery and murder in Brockton, Massachusetts. Their trial received national attention as defense attorney, Fred Moore, veteran of legal battles for the radical IWW, focused on what he considered a class struggle between a Bostonian, white, Anglo-Saxon Protestant majority versus an immigrant, Catholic, Italian minority. The American intellectual community followed Moore's lead and protested the trial, but in the end the publicity probably did more damage than good, since the carnival aspect of the trial tended to cloud the issues and mislead a confused jury that found the two men guilty. They were executed on August 23, 1927, which for many, like Edna St. Vincent Millay, was a day when American honor died.

Intellectual protest, shaped by the above events, developed along two lines: some became a renunciation of the American industrial age that seemed to have generated a world war and now subverted the values of peacetime America; and some evolved as a literature of chaos that expressed disenchantment with life and the disorder of contemporary society. At the Liberal Club on Macdougal Street in the Village, or in *The Masses*, a radical newspaper with its headquarters in a converted store on Greenwich Avenue, or at the Roundtable at the Algonquin Hotel—one could hear poets, writers, artist, and performers express themselves along these lines.

The last area where change rapidly occurred was in the mores of the Nation. During the War, many women had worked in factories or had served through The National League of Women's Service by driving staff cars and ambulances in the City. These women were little inclined to surrender their new-found emancipation once the War came to an end. During the 1920's an ever-increasing number of women attended college, entered into the job market, and married later in life. Fashions changed. Hair was bobbed and dyed, eyebrows plucked and penciled, cheeks and lips rouged, and hemlines rose to the strains of a popular tune, "I'll Say She Does." A moral revolution was in the making, and the "new woman" was bent on leading her own life free from the social restraints faced by her mother.

But the ease with which the new woman stepped into a new set of values was indigenous of society in general. Ever since the passing of Prohibition on January 16, 1920, a growing disrespect for the laws of the land, with an insurgence in organized crime, had developed nationwide. By the mid-1920's over thirty thousand speak-easys were serving countless patrons from all ranks of society. In the dangerous dives known as clip-joints, cab-joints, or steer-joints, an unwary customer could find himself at best with his pockets picked by night's end, or, at worst, in the City Morgue from drinking whiskey tainted with wood alcohol. In the better-class brownstone speak-easys, operated as "clubs," one could purchase imported Scotch or gin. One of the more exotic places was the 21-Club, boasting two bars and restaurants, a dance-floor with orchestra, lounges for conversation, game rooms for ping-pong, backgammon and mah-jong, and an elaborate electrical security system that in the event of a raid could make sections of walls turn and disappear.

The principal objective when attending these speak-easies was, in the words of Ford Maddox Ford, "to have a good time." The mood was infectious and spread throughout the City where the "good time" was so sacred, Ford noted, "you may be excused anything you do in searching for it."[13] Organized crime grew rapidly, supplying the speak-easies with illicit alcohol for thousands of eager customers, many of whom had probably never taken a drink before Prohibition. It became fun to break the law, and everyone did it. Consequently, the crimes of bootleggers were applauded by most who considered them modern-day Robin Hoods, flaunting the laws that everyone despised. As the revenues from bootlegging increased, organized crime entered other areas. Among the notables of the 1920's in New York City were Larry Fay, whose control extended into the milk industry, Louis "Lepke" Buchalter, and Jacob "Gurrah" Shapiro, who controlled the garment and fur industry and later controlled the baking, trucking, and movie industry. The most flamboyant mobster was Francesco

Castiglia, alias Frank Costello, who organized a gathering of the clans in Atlantic City for establishing a sense of harmony and territorial order within the crime families on the East Coast.

In a league with Costello was the colorful figure of Mayor Jimmie Walker. Walker, for many, was a personification of the times. Handsome, debonair, a man who loved the social perks of his job but none of the hard work, who saw nothing questionable in having his exorbitant hotel bills, tailor bills, and other personal expenses paid for by wealthy benefactors who basked under his largess, a man who rarely rose before noon to conduct any official business, and who preferred frequenting nightclubs into the early morning hours—for many, Walker was representative of what New Yorkers considered themselves to be. If doubts appeared about his capability or questions were raised concerning widespread political corruption, he was quick with the flippant wisecrack or a glib comeback that stiffled the opposition. Reformers, he once joked, were people who went through sewers in glass-bottomed boats. The crowds loved him, and so did organized crime. Under Walker's protective umbrella of municipal corruption, organized crime became profitable on a scale never before realized. Through political allies, gangsters reached into every aspect of the City government controlling the police, public prosecutors, magistrates, judges in the higher courts, and a large number of administrative officials. Everyone, from newspapers down to the man-on-the-street, accepted the Walker Administration. Political corruption was merely another expression of the happy times, and the gaiety, tolerance, and carelessness would remain, in the words of Ford Maddox Ford, like a "storming-party hurrying towards an unknown goal," until it all came to an end with the Crash of 1929.

Manhattan Transfer stands eminently among the novels of the 1920's in its attempt to capture that era within an American city. The City that concerns Dos Passos is New York, and though the novel covers a time span from the late 1890's to the mid-1920's, the views it expresses and the characters it presents are primarily reflective of Manhattan during the Walker years. Sinclair Lewis appreciated this quality in the novel and praised its "breathless reality, . . . its flashes, its cutbacks, its speed" in presenting the modern city. Dos Passos rejected the traditional stylistic route of

earlier city novelists, and instead presents a kaleidescopic panorama of disparate scenes and characters that eventually collide
with each other during the course of the plot. Within this confusion is mirrored the haphazardness of city life. For Lewis, the new
style represented "the foundation of a whole new school of novel
writing." "Dos Passos," he concluded, "*may* be, more than Dreiser,
Cather, Hergesheimer, Cabell, or Anderson, the father of human-
ized and living fiction."[14]

Yet, despite its complex development, the novel presents a
tightly organized overview of the City. For Dos Passos the City
exists on two levels: the physical and the psychological. The physical is the most obvious. This is the City that preoccupied Wharton
and Crane—the City of changing dimensions and neighborhoods.
In *Manhattan Transfer* the City continues to grow at a frantic pace,
and has now spread beyond Manhattan onto Long Island. The
birth of megalopolis is on the horizon. New Yorkers are now an
aggressively mobile lot who clog the City streets with their shiny
new automobiles on every Sunday afternoon:

> Motors purring hot, exhausts reeking, cars from Babylon and Ja-
> maica, cars from Montauk, Port Jefferson, Patchogue, limousines
> from Long Beach, Far Rockaway, roadsters from Great Neck—cars
> full of asters and wet bathingsuits, sunsinged necks, mouths sticky
> from sodas and hotdawgs . . . cars dusted with pollen of ragweed
> and goldenrod.[15]

In this city, the senses are assaulted continually. Manhattan, for
Dos Passos, is far too physically complex to be completely absorbed at any one moment. It is too much in motion. The trainyard
outside the Merivale apartment, the cars incessantly buzzing by
the Thatcher residence, the repeated image of rushing fire
engines—all enhance and underline this terrible restlessness of
city life. One can only achieve a brief glimpse of the passing scene.
Sometimes the focus is on the visual, and the City becomes a city
of moving lights as it does in one description of the night:

> All night the great buildings stand quiet and empty, their million
> windows dark. Drooling light the ferries chew tracks across the lac-
> quered harbor. At midnight the fourfunneled express steamers slide
> into the dark out of their glary berths. Bankers blearyeyed from
> secret conferences hear the hooting of the tugs as they are let out of
> side doors by lightningbug watchmen; they settle grunting into the

back seats of limousines, and are whisked uptown into the Forties, clinking streets of ginwhite whiskey-yellow ciderfizzling lights. (p. 305)

Sometimes sounds and smells dominate as they do in one scene where Jimmy Herf lies awake on his bed conscious of the summertime City around him:

The faraway sounds of sirens from the river gave him gooseflesh. From the street he heard footsteps, the sound of men and women's voices, low youthful laughs of people going home two by two. A phonograph was playing *Secondhand Rose*. He lay on his back on top of the sheet. There came on the air through the window a sourness of garbage, a smell of burnt gasoline and traffic and dusty pavements, a huddled stuffiness of pigeonhole rooms where men and women's bodies writhed alone tortured by the night and the young summer. (p. 194)

The City's rapid expansion and overwhelming physical presence creates other problems of perception. Appearance becomes more important than substance in this transitory City. Friendship and business relationships rise and fall as quickly as city buildings; superficiality predominates. When Bud Korpenning arrives in the City, his immediate desire is to get "to the center of things." But he never achieves his objective, for the "center" remains as hidden and enigmatic as every aspect of city life. The out-of-towner is hopelessly doomed if such is his intention. Early in the novel a friendly short-order cook attempts to set Bud straight concerning getting ahead in the City:

I'm goin to slip you a bit of advice, feller, and it won't cost you nutten. You go an git a shave and a haircut and brush the hayseeds out o yer suit a bit before you start lookin. You'll be more likely to git somethin. It's looks that count in this city. (p. 5)

But Bud fails to understand the man's advice, preferring instead to believe in his own abilities and thereby dooming himself to frustration and certain failure. Bud's dilemma affects all city dwellers to some extent and certainly newcomers such as himself. Success is largely determined by one's ability to "keep up appearances" and present a good facade. Sensitive or perceptive characters, such as

Jimmy Herf, eventually find the City too much to handle and have to leave it in order to keep their sanity. Those who remain and succeed are excellent symbol-handlers.

Jimmy's relatives, the Merivales, are a good example of the successful urbanite. Dressed in a dark gray suit with a faint green stripe in it, an olive green knitted necktie fastened by a small gold nugget stickpin, olive green woolen socks with black clockmarks and dark red Oxford shoes, "their laces neatly tied with doubleknots that never came undone," James Merivale presents an image of conservative upper middle-class respectability. (p. 309) This, of course, is his intention for he well realizes that proper dress is the prerequisite of business success. Certain codes must be followed. He drops off carrying a cane because "the younger men down there don't carry them," only vice presidents. He does not want to be overdressed for his position in the business community. (pp. 309-310)

Appearance transcends substance in religious matters too. The commonplace religion of Mrs. Culveteer, Mr. Thatcher's neighbor, is devoid of spiritual regeneration and desiccate of moral guidance. She finds her pastor, Mr. Lourton, most appealing in that his sermons are absent of a tiresome moral tone. "It's really more like attending an intensely interesting lecture than going to church . . .," she informs Thatcher who prefers to "lay around the house Sunday." (p. 199)

In a similar vein, Thatcher's daughter Ellen gravitates toward and succeeds in a profession whose principal function is creating illusion—acting. A realist at heart, Ellen sometimes finds her role-playing aggravating: "I hate it; it's all false," she confides in her producer, Harry Goldweiser. "Sometimes I want to run down to the foots and tell the audience, go home you damn fools. This is a rotten show a lot of fake acting and you ought to know it." Her exasperation, however, falls on deaf ears. Goldweiser, a symbol-handling New Yorker, nudges a nearby friend: "Didn't I tell ye she was nuts, Sol? Didn't I tell ye she was nuts?" (p. 212)

In a city where appearance becomes more important than substance, mankind inevitably sinks to a dehumanized level of existence. Dos Passos repeatedly emphasizes the brutalization of the City's inhabitants, their loss of identity and absorption into the concrete uniformity of Manhattan. The commuters who appear at the very beginning of the novel cascade through the "Manuresmelling wooden tunnel of the ferryhouse, crushed and jostling like apples fed down a chute into a press." (p. 3) In another passage an infant is described repulsively as "a knot of earthworms." (p. 3)

But there are other causes for the dehumanization of the city-man. There is the general confusion and speed of city life that strips man of his ability to relax and contemplate his position in things. Lunch becomes a frantic affair where people "eat hurriedly without looking at each other, with their eyes on their plates, in their cups." (p. 314) Diners become way stations for the "jostling crowds filing in and out the subway through the drabgreen gloom." (p. 314) Finally, there are the harsh working environments such as the dress shop where Anna works: "a long low room with long tables down the middle piled with silk and crepe fabrics. . . . bowed heads auburn, blond, black, brown of girls sewing." (p. 346)

Each of the novel's principal characters, therefore, no matter how economically successful, is inevitably destroyed within the confines of the City. Unhappy in love and life, Ellen retreats into a "hypothetical dollself" where she becomes as "rigid as a porcelain figure. . . ." (pp. 374-375) "She had made up her mind. It seemed as if she had set a photograph of herself in her own place, forever frozen into a single gesture. An invisible silk band of bitterness was tightening round her throat, strangling." (p. 375) Her lover, Stan Emery, also finds himself trapped within a city that cannot tolerate his eccentricities. At first he withdraws, like Ellen, into a dehumanized shell, "kerist I wish I was a skyscraper" (p. 252), and ends up burning himself to death.

But the New York landscape presented in *Manhattan Transfer* is not restricted to the physical, for it encompasses a psychological dimension as well. On the psychological level, New York City stands preeminently as the city of dreams, and if anything lends to the City a sense of vitality it is this trait. Ironically, it stands apart from the physical City (in that each New Yorker dreams his own dream of the City), yet is inexorably linked to the City's massive dimensions that fire the imagination. In "Metropolis" Dos Passos draws the connection between the physical and the psychological when he establishes a link between modern New York and the great cities of antiquity:

There were Babylon and Nineveh; they were built of brick. Athens was gold marble columns. Rome was held up on broad arches of rubble. In Constantinople the minarets flame like great candles round the Golden Horn . . . Steel, glass, tile, concrete will be the materials of the skyscrapers. Crammed on the narrow island the millionwindowed buildings will jut glittering, pyramid on pyramid like the white cloudhead above a thunderstorm. (p. 12)

In a later chapter, "Nickelodeon," the surprising buying power of a nickel in the greatest commercial city in the western world allows for dreams:

A nickel before midnight buys tomorrow . . . holdup headlines, a cup of coffee in the automat, a ride to Woodlawn, Fort Lee, Flatbush. . . . A nickel in the slot buys chewing gum. Somebody Loves Me, Baby Divine, You're in Kentucky Juss Shu' As You're Born . . . bruised notes of foxtrots go limping out of doors, blues, waltzes (We'd Danced the Whole Night Through) trail gyrating tinsel memories. . . . (p. 291)

Between these passages a host of people pass through the novel, each with his or her own particular city-inspired dream catering to his or her own particular outlook. New York is different things to different people.

The immigrants are one group of people who possess a specific dream of the City. For some, New York symbolizes the dream of regeneration, a city where the old customs and fashions can be dropped forever and a new man emerge, free for a second chance at life and success. At the end of "Ferry Slip," we encounter a small, bearded, bandylegged man in a derby walking up Allen Street. Evidently dejected and depressed, he is oblivious to the "annihilating clatter" of overhead trains and the "rancid sweet huddled smell of packed tenements." Suddenly his attention is riveted by a drugstore window presenting a green advertising card on which are the clean-shaven features and "dollarproud" eyes of King C. Gillette. Inspired by the image of material success presented in the advertisement, the bearded man buys a razor, returns home and shaves off his beard, much to the consternation of his wife and children. He is adamant: "Vat's a matter? Dont ye like it?" as he walks back and forth "with the safety razor shining in his hands now and then gently fingering his smooth chin." (p. 11) He has achieved in his own way a part of the American dream.

A few pages later, the dream is expressed again in the character of Emile, a French sailor intent upon making America his new home. "I want to get somewhere in the world, that's what I mean," he tells a friend, "Europe's rotten and stinking. In America a fellow can get ahead. Birth dont matter, education dont matter. It's all getting ahead." (p. 21) Similar sentiments are also echoed in Chapter Three, "Dollars," by a young man discussing with his father the reason for immigrant migration to America:

> "I'd give a million dollars," said the old man resting on his oars, "to know what they come for."
> "Just for that pop," said the young man who sat in the stern. "Ain't it the land of opportoonity?"
> "One thing I do know," said the old man. "When I was a boy it was wild Irish came in the spring with the first run of shad. . . . Now there aint no more shad, an them folks, Lord knows where they come from."
> "It's the land of opportoonity." (p. 49)

What the young man realizes, and the old man cannot, is that it is the City's power over the imagination and not its physical presence that now acts as a magnet on the world.

Ed Thatcher is not an immigrant, and his dreams, also fostered by the City, are of a different sort. His dreams are the dreams of a second generation of Americans whose vistas are now bordered by the commonplace values of a rising middle class. Thatcher's basic dream is to become an honored member of the business community and a stellar accountant. Upon reading a newspaper article on New York's becoming the world's second largest metropolis, he folds the paper and daydreams about his becoming a junior partner in his firm. This dream, like all of Thatcher's dreams, however, comes to an abrupt end. A piece of china is knocked off the bookcase while he is engaging in a bow to an imagined audience. Evidently Thatcher's dreams are limited by both his physical and mental capacity as well as his middle-class outlook on life.

Speculators and investors have a different dream of the City. Some, like the unnamed real estate developer in "Metropolis," view New York as a symbol of capitalist expansion and progress:

> A great deal is going to happen in the next few years. All these mechanical inventions—telephones, electricity, steel bridges, horseless vehicles—they are all leading somewhere. It's up to us to be on the inside, in the forefront of progress. . . . (p. 15)

Others like Phil Sandborne, however, have visions of a "purified" city of steel and glass, possessing a divine architecture that inspires man to a new dimension of human existence. For Sandborne, the City of the future would have buildings. . .

> ornamented with vivid colors. Imagine bands of scarlet round the entablatures of skyscrapers. Colored tile would revolutionize the whole life of the city. . . . Instead of fallin back on the orders or on gothic or romanesque decorations we could evolve new designs, new colors, new forms. If there was a little color in the town all this hardshell inhibited life'd break down. . . . There'd be more love an less divorce. . . . (p. 257)

Sandborne is not the only visionary in the novel, however.

Rosie, the daughter of Thatcher's Jewish neighbor, envisions the City as a place where a woman can liberate herself from the domestic tyranny that plagued women in the old world. Unhappily married to a violent husband, she cannot accept her mother's advice to bear the burden of a wife, remembering that, "married life ain't all beer and skittles. . . ." "I won't go back to the dirty brute," she answers, "this ain't Russia; it's little old New York. A girl's got some rights here." (p. 22) Rosie's dream is the dream of a liberated woman, and New York City has given her the ability to believe in this dream.

Other visionaries abound. There is Marco, the anarchist, who believes that the City will soon become a battleground upon which will be built a modern Utopia, a place where, "You will walk out in the street and the police will run away, you will go into a bank and there will be money poured out on the floor and you wont stoop to pick it up, no more good. . . ." (pp. 38-39) Finally, there is Anna, the seamstress, and her boyfriend Elmer who anticipate a socialistic horizon of fair wages and decent housing for all.

Unfortunately, many similarly minded characters in *Manhattan Transfer* are eventually subverted by the economic demands of the City. They lose their earlier idealism and often degenerate into a cult of the self. Consequently, there is a certain element of moral perplexity in *Manhattan Transfer*. Dos Passos, like most of his generation, had become disillusioned with the "inherent nobility" of man after experiencing and witnessing the atrocities of World War I. The nineteenth-century vision of man as an advanced species was sufficiently deflated by the mass genocide of trench warfare. The grand illusion was diffused as grim realities came to light. These revelations precipitated an aggressive socialism after the War of which Dos Passos was a part. He and others felt that something had to be done—laws proposed, legislation passed—that would save the common man from being manipulated by powerful interest groups into future wholesale butchery. Unlike many fellow Americans, he viewed the business boom of the 1920's, and especially that of New York's, with a jaundiced eye, for it seemed to incorporate much of the greed and aggressiveness characteristic of the Great War. Progress was alluring, but what were the future costs? Ideals could be subverted.

In a letter to a friend during the early part of the decade, he noted his ambivalence: "New York—after all—is magnificent, a city of cavedwellers, with a frightful, brutal ugliness about it. . . . People swarm meekly like ants along designated routes, crushed by the disdainful and pitiless things around them." For him, the City has become the modern "Nineveh and Babylon, or Ur of the Chalders, of the immense cities which loom like balisks behind the horizon in ancient Jewish tales, where the temples rose as high as mountains and people ran trembling through dirty little alleys to the constant noise of whips with hilts of gold."[16] This is a city that can easily create and subvert dreams.

Subversion is often generated by the frantic cosmopolitan atmosphere of the City. In this environment, the dreamer finds himself alone and often reduced to brutish instincts or even suicide. Bud Korpenning's dream to be in the center of things becomes a hopeless search set against the dismal urban panorama of sterile growth and decay:

> With a long slow stride, limping a little from his blistered feet, Bud walked down Broadway, past empty lots where tin cans glittered among grass and sumach bushes and ragweed, between ranks of billboards and Bull Durham signs, past shanties and abandoned squatters' shacks, past gulches heaped with wheelscarred rubbishpiles where dumpcarts were dumping ashes and clinkers, past knobs of gray outcrop where steamdrills continually tapped and nibbled, past excavations out of which wagons full of rock and clay toiled up plank roads to the street. . . . (pp. 23-24)

The people he meets in this wasteland are equally repugnant and offensive. There are the ever-present, cold-hearted watchmen and police detectives in derby hats; the butcherboy who responds to Bud's question for a job with a laugh, "Kerist I thought you was goin to ask for a handout. . . . I guess you aint a Newyorker" (p. 25); and the avaricious landlady who reneges on her promise to pay him a dollar for hauling coal and threatens him with the law if he protests. Bud never achieves his goal of finding the "center" of things because in this City there is no center, no heart, in its anatomy—only a hardened shell of callousness. Suicide marks the end of his fruitless journey.

Bud's failure is typical of the fate of each character in the novel who finds himself isolated and rejected, a victim of the City's obsessive cult of the self. Neither success or failure has any effect on the city dweller's lonliness. George Baldwin rises to become a leading figure in the world of law and politics, but he confides to Ellen Thatcher that the "terrible thing about having New York go stale on you is that there's nowhere else. It's the top of the world. All we can do is go round and round in a squirrel cage." (p. 220) His excessive philandering is more than mere licentiousness. It is a perverse reflection of his need to establish a lasting relationship. Like Bud, he too wants to get at the "center of things," and like Bud, he fails. At the other end of the economic scale is Joe Harland, the former millionaire and "King of the curb," who now, at forty-five, finds himself without friends or money. Rejected by even his family and finding solace only in alcoholism, he is a reminder of the City's cruelty and the city dweller's lonliness.

Between the extremes of Baldwin and Harland are the numerous representatives of the middle class, equally lonely. Ellen Thatcher seeks isolation after leaving her husband Oglethorpe. At a hotel, her bed becomes a "raft on which she was marooned alone, always alone, afloat on a growling ocean." (p. 168) Herf envisions city lovers in "pigeonhole bedrooms, tangled sleepers twisted and strangled like the roots of potbound plants." (p. 235) Surrounding Jimmie and Ellen are the numerous, nameless, colorless, amorphous shopgirls and salesmen who people the novel, frequenting movie houses or cafes, with "faces decomposed into a graygreen blur." (p. 155)

The cult of the self in the City creates other problems. It fosters aggressive competitiveness, prejudice, and selfishness in many of the characters. Jimmy's successful Uncle, Jeff Merivale, is an excessively competitive man whose lifestyle is totally governed by his own sense of greed. For Uncle Jeff only one goal exists—to attain a position in the business community sufficient enough to allow one to dine at a club where "the wealthiest and the most successful men in the country eat lunch. . . ." (p. 118) Distressed by his nephew's apparent lack of interest in "moneymatters," he dines him at a businessman's club with the intention of instilling in him a sense of "enthusiasm about earning your living, making good in a man's world."

> Look around you. . . . Thrift and enthusiasm has made these men what they are. It's made me, put me in the position to offer you the comfortable home, the cultured surroundings that I do offer you. . . . I realize that your education has been a little peculiar . . . but the really formative period of your life is beginning. Now's the time to take a brace and lay the foundations of your future career. . . . (p. 119)

Of course Herf has little interest in a lifestyle of such limited upper middle-class dimensions.

Prejudice results when each individual sees himself pitted against a pitiless city and its inhabitants. Marco, the anarchist, having lived in New York City for a number of years, finds it a battlefront of class warfare. "I'm fed up with this rotten town," he expostulates to the recently arrived Emile and Congo. "It's the same all over the world, the police beating us up, rich people cheating us out of . . . starvation wages, and who's fault? . . . Dio cane!" Marco's anarchism is logical to a point, but his growing rage against injustice makes his rhetoric degenerate into a maniacal frenzy of hatred: "God's on their side, like a policeman," he continues, "when the day comes we'll kill God. . . . I am an anarchist." (p. 37) Consequently, the underlying idealism of his argument is choked by a fierce paranoia generated by his overly sensitive nature. Like many other characters in the novel, he ends up on a narrow track of logic, scrupulously and savagely defending his own position, unable to understand Emile's moderate view that "People are all the same. It's only that some people get ahead and others dont. . . ." (p. 37)

A different brand of prejudice finds its way into the Merivale family, that has a generous amount of distaste for the City's ethnic groups. A bastion of WASP integrity, they consider themselves as combatants against the changing values of an ever-changing city, "overrun with kikes and low Irish . . .," as Uncle Jeff complains.

"In ten years a Christian wont be able to make a living. . . . I tell you the Catholics and the Jews are going to run us out of our own country, that's what they are going to do." (p. 101) A similar mentality is found at the end of the novel in the character of an unnamed Philadelphian who brains a fellow citizen who has the effrontery to wear a straw hat "out of season." (p. 401) Paradoxically, it is the cult of the self that has generated this fascist type of conformity; it is a selfish attitude that fails to understand or tolerate the values of others.

Finally, there is the cult's influence on the general decay of morality between men and women. Healthy, happy men-women relationships are rare in *Manhattan Transfer*, and when they do appear, such as in the case of Dutch and Francie, or Congo and Nevada, it is far too bizarre to qualify as an example of the middle-class norm. The traditional roles of men and women have broken down within this environment of selfish pursuit.

Part of this dilemma is symbolized in Ellen's overtly masculine temperament that rejects the traditional values of femininity. As a child, she significantly harps on her desire to be a boy and sacrifices her adult life to this wish. Strong-willed and possessed of a consummate ability to take charge of a situation, she disarms a burglar who breaks into her apartment, walks out on her first husband, and gets a job when her second husband, Jimmy Herf, becomes unemployed. Jimmy, a sentimentalist, searches for a feminine tenderness in Ellen but instead finds "an intricate machine of sawtooth steel whitebright bluebright copperbright in his arms." (p. 228) Her brief flirtation with femininity is reserved for Stan Emery, a confused alcoholic and ne'er-do-well destined for a short life. His strong sexual attraction to her is largely instinctive and animalistic, without understanding or reason.

The love affair between Cassie and Morris is similarly tragic. Cassie is not a twentieth-century woman. In many ways she fulfills the traditional role of women during the late nineteenth century. She is an idealist—a person devoted to the purity and beauty of "true love." Her beau, Morris, is an uninspired example of male ego, sexually aggressive, dominant, and frequently insensitive. As can be expected, their relationship ends in failure with neither understanding the motives or desires of the other.

Throughout the novel, countless other characters appear who reflect this spiritual decay of love. Casual relationships between men and women are frequently brutal and described in violent, disharmonious terms rife with sharp, jagged imagery:

> Under the arclight that spluttered pink and green-edged violet the man in the checked suit passed two girls. The full-lipped oval face of the girl nearest to him; her eyes were like aknifethrust. He walked a few paces then turned and followed them fingering his new satin necktie. He made sure the horseshoe diamond pin was firm in its place. (p. 61)

A young man in a straw hat and driving a red Stutz roadster confronts Ellen on a city street during a summer day:

> His eyes twinkled in hers, he jerked back his head smiling an upsidedown smile, pursing his lips so that they seemed to brush her cheek. He pulled the lever of the brake and opened the door with the other hand. She snapped her eyes away and walked on with her chin up. (p. 137)

In each instance relations between men and women have been reduced to the purely physical. Consequently, abortion becomes a dominant issue in the novel and is made penetratingly graphic in a scene related by Alice Sheffield to her boyfriend:

> O Buck I have the most horrible thing to tell you. It made me deathly ill. . . . You know what I told you about the awful smell we had in the apartment we thought was rats? This morning I met the woman who lives on the ground floor. . . . O it makes me sick to think of it. Her face was green as that bus. . . . It seems they've been having the plumbing examined by an inspector. . . . They arrested the woman upstairs. O it's too disgusting. I cant tell you about it. . . . I'll never go back there. I'd die if I did. . . . There wasnt a drop of water in the house all day yesterday. (p. 378)

Water, a symbol of regeneration and growth, has been turned off in the apartment house as the plumbers remove their ghastly discovery from the drain pipes.

The institution of marriage concomitantly suffers. The sterile marriage of Ellen Thatcher and John Oglethorpe is foreshadowed during their honeymoon, as their train passes through New Jersey on its way to Atlantic City:

> she could only look out at the brown marshes and the million black windows of factories and the puddly streets of towns and a rusty steamboat in a canal and barns and Bull Durham signs and round-

faced Spearmint gnomes all barred and crisscrossed with bright flaws of rain. (p. 116)

They are not alone. Ellen's parents were equally incompatible; her father was a timid man, her mother a neurotic hypochondriac. A taximan driving Ellen to a hotel after her final breakup with Oglethorpe commiserates with her situation. He has recently left his own wife:

> I aint goin back to her an I aint goin to support her no more. . . . She can put me in jail if she likes. I'm troo. I'm gettin an apartment on Twentysecond Avenoo wid another feller an we're goin to git a pianer an live quiet an lay offen the skoits. (pp. 167-168)

Herf enters into his marriage with Ellen "paralyzed like in a nightmare; she was a porcelaine figure under a bellglass." (p. 300) Nellie McNeil cheats on her husband with George Baldwin who is equally unfaithful to his own wife. The list goes on, and in each instance the cause is the same—the cult of the self.

Without love the family unit also suffers. The lack of communication between parents and children begins at birth. Susie Thatcher rejects her baby, Ellen, when she is unable to recognize it in the hospital, just as Ellen will later reject her own after an affair with Emery. Nellie McNeil neglects her children during her clandestine affair. Conversely, children reject their parents. Bud Korpenning runs away from his stepparent; Ellen rarely visits her father during his retirement; Stan has been estranged from his father for years; Jimmy Herf has never really known his father except as a "dark" image out of the past, and his adopted parents, the Merivale's, are to him repulsive.

Sibling rivalry further disrupts the family. Herf is at odds with his surrogate brother and sister, Jim and Ellen Merivale—a pattern witnessed among lesser characters in the book. Mike O'Keefe quarrels with his brother Joe after the latter becomes a wardheeler. Mike complains:

> you been pickin on me worsen the old man. I'm glad I aint goin to stay round this goddam town long. It's enough to drive a feller cookoo. If I can get on some kind of a tub that puts to sea before the *Golden Gate* by God I'm going to do it. (p. 239)

For many characters like Mike there is little in New York City life to encourage a stable family unit. The City's constant economic and physical mobility creates stresses, which along with the hedonistic age, doom the family to a certain death.

The growing trend toward lawlessness in the City during the 1920's is also due to the cult of the self. Crime, both petty and organized, as well as political corruption, appear sporadically in the novel as insidious and invisible threats to the characters. But criminals, themselves, are not villains or perverted expressions of the American dream preying upon the unwary. Sometimes the criminal is even an understanding, compassionate, and appealing figure. A good example is Congo Jake.

Congo, whose real name remains unknown, surfaces now and again throughout the novel and at the end appears as "Armand Duval," a wealthy bootlegger. An ironic comment on the American success story, Congo represents a criminal element that has evolved "naturally" out of the times. He has been a sailor most of his life, has worked as a bartender, has connections, and, consequently, enters into the highly profitable field of bootlegging. He has no strong desire to be a criminal, but he does want to be comfortable, and bootlegging offers such a life. In this sense he "naturally" falls into it.

Congo is appealing in that he never loses his intrinsic kindness and sensitivity along the way. This is evident in his lasting friendship with Jimmy Herf. Congo never scorns his former friends, and he has no illusions about himself. He merely wants a slice of the good life and altruistically wants others, whether Jimmy Herf or consumers of his bootlegged wares, to share in his general success. In a novel filled with the egotistical, he is a refreshing change. When we last encounter him, we can wholeheartedly concur with Herf's assessment: "Congo. . . . I mean Armand, if I'd been God and had to decide who in this city should make a million dollars and who shouldn't I swear you're the man I should have picked." (p. 383)

Although he appears only briefly in the novel, nobility is clearly evident in another racketeer—Jake Silverman. On the surface he is simply another small-time gangster and confidence man, flashily dressed, vain, and apparently unfaithful to his girlfriend. But he belies this image at the time of his arrest by federal agents when he shows his true feelings toward her:

> Almost immediately he was gone, followed by the two detectives with a satchel full of letters. His kiss was still wet on her lips. She

looked dazedly round the empty deathly quiet room. She noticed some writing on the lavender blotter on the desk. It was his hand-writing, very scrawly: Hock everything and beat it; you are a good kid. Tears began running down her cheeks. She sat a long while with her head dropped on the desk kissing the penciled words on the blotter. (pp. 349-350)

Like Congo, Silverman exhibits a character that sets him above other men—both within and outside the law.

The ambiguity of criminals such as Congo and Silverman cre-ates a very vague distinction between the lawless and the law-abiding in New York City. While the criminal may be possessed of gentlemanly and generous attributes, conversely, the average gen-tleman can also exhibit a touch of the larcenous. When Jimmy and Ellen return from Europe, they deliberately flaunt the laws of their country by smuggling in imported liquor. On a smaller scale, they engage in the same activity that sustains Congo Jake. But there is a difference. While Congo breaks the law in order to make a living, the Herf's break the law merely to break the law. It is this distinc-tion that makes their act intrinsically more disgusting and hypo-critical in the long run than the blatantly honest bootlegging of Congo Jake.

Another type of criminal is encountered in the corrupt figures of Gus McNeil and George Baldwin. Both pose as distinguished men of society—one as a powerful politician and labor leader, the other as a prominent lawyer. McNeil, "bullnecked redfaced with a heavy watchchain in his vest . . . pulling on his cigar," is every inch the wheeler-dealer politician of the 1920's, having risen to his present position as an alderman from his early days as a truck driver. He knows people—their weak points, the power of a bribe or a returned favor—and is involved during the course of the novel in a series of shady deals involving business contracts and bonds. When things get rough, he goes to his old friend and legal adviser, Baldwin, who is able to control the reformers who question McNeil's motives. "Well aint they friends of yours?," he asks Baldwin; "You can fix it up with em." (p. 205)

Yet despite their obvious hypocrisy, Gus McNeil and George Baldwin are not villainous. Towards the end of the novel, it be-comes evident that they are only another example of their age, generated by the overall corruption in the City and the Nation. The support that Baldwin and McNeil receive from the powerful members of the business community, like Deusch, clearly indicates the mainspring of their corruption. Deusch represents the central malaise of a post-War America, a blind capitalism geared only toward the profit motive and fearful of anything that will undermine those profits. As Deusch points out to Baldwin and McNeil . . .

> the country is going through a dangerous period of reconstruction . . . the confusion attendant on the winding up of great conflict . . . the bankruptcy of a continent . . . bolshevism and subversive doctrines rife . . . America. . . . America . . . is in the position of taking over the receivership of the world. The great principles of democracy, of that commercial freedom upon which our whole civilization depends are more than ever at stake. (pp. 287-288)

Of course, the key words are "commercial freedom." Social freedoms and civil liberties are non-existent phrases in Deusch's vocabulary. People such as Deusch have made a mockery of the American legal system, orienting it toward their own narrow business interests. They have corrupted the police and court judges who protect those who have power from those who are powerless. A good example is the "white fishfaced" conservative judge with nose glasses who sentences the petty criminals, Francie and Dutch, to twenty years each for their modest burglaries, while remaining oblivious to the far more devastating circles of organized crime within the City. From his lips fall the platitudes of his generation:

> Not that I dont feel as a tender and loving father the misfortunes, the lack of education and ideals, the lack of a loving home and tender care of a mother that has led this young woman into a life of immorality and misery, led away by the temptations of cruel and voracious men and the excitement and wickedness of what has been too well named, the jazz age. Yet at the moment when these thoughts are about to temper with mercy the stern anger of the law, the importunate recollection rises of other young girls, perhaps hundreds of them at this moment in this great city about to fall . . . and I remember that mercy misplaced is often cruelty in the long run . . . . (pp. 391-392)

Even intellectual circles have become self-centered and a reflection of the City's narcissism. The artist is often divorced from cultural heritages, preferring instead to experiment with exotic themes and styles, no matter how bizarre. In such an atmosphere of artistic license, a false intellectualism predominates. Mrs. Voorhees' party in "Revolving Doors" exhibits the new line:

> The record on the phonograph was Turkish. Hester Voorhees, a skinny woman with a mop of hennaed hair cut short at the level of her ears, came out holding a pot of drawling incense out in front of her preceded by two young men who unrolled a carpet as she came. She wore silk bloomers and a clinking metal girdle and brassieres. Every body was clapping and saying, "How wonderful, how marvelous,". . . . (p. 341)

By the end of the novel, such parties degenerate into drunken numbness, an example being the "farewell" party Jimmy attends before leaving New York City for good:

> The long front room was full of ginbottles, gingerale bottles, ashtrays crowded with halfsmoked cigarettes, couples dancing, people sprawled on sofas. Endlessly the phonograph played Lady . . . lady be good. A glass of gin was pushed into Herf's hand. A girl came up to him. . . . Herf took the hand of the girl beside him and made her dance with him. She kept stumbling over his feet. He danced her round until he was opposite to the halldoor; he opened the door and foxtrotted her out into the hall. Mechanically she put up her mouth to be kissed. He kissed her quickly and reached for his hat. (pp. 401–402)

The intellectual climate of the City, like everything else, has become so preoccupied with its own self-image that only a crass hedonism can prevail.

How then does one survive these damning influences of the City during the 1920's? The answer rests with three characters who seem to have the most control over their environment—Congo Jake, Nevada Jones, and Jimmy Herf. Congo and Nevada survive by becoming as amorphous as their various names imply. Congo shifts from occupation to occupation through a myriad of aliases. Nevada (named for the state in which she was born and where her mother at the time was filing a divorce) becomes, respectively, California Jones, a prostitute, a psychological advisor for a disturbed homosexual, and, at last count, Congo's "girl." Nor do Congo and Nevada exhibit preconceived assumptions about life and people. They accept each day as it comes and are aptly suited for city living. Congo, for example, cannot understand the fine nuances of Herf's logic, a logic that makes life in the City unbearable. "Mister 'Erf," he warns Jimmy, "you tink too much." (p. 384) The materialistic values of the City represent for Congo all that one needs to attain in life. Why question it? But for Herf, a representative of a second generation upper middle class New York, something more is needed to make life satisfying. As he warns Congo,

> The difference between you and me is that you're going up in the social scale, Armand, and I'm going down . . . When you were a messboy on a steamboat I was a horrid little chalkyfaced kid living at the Ritz. My mother and father did all this Vermont marble black-walnut grand Babylonian stuff . . . there's nothing more for me to do about it. . . . If I thought it'd be any good to me I swear I've got the energy to sit up and make a million dollars. But I get no organic sensation out of that stuff any more. I've got to have something new, different. . . . Your sons'll be like that Congo. . . . (pp. 383-384)

For Herf, another life and higher goals beyond the influence of the City are needed. But what these goals specifically are remains cloudy. What is certain is that within the confines of New York, life is too fast to be understood clearly, too hectic to be truly appreciated, and too selfish to be kind.

Chapter Three

[1]Bayrd Still, *Mirror for Gotham: New York As Seen By Contemporaries from Dutch Days to the Present* (New York: New York University Press, 1956), p. 258.

[2]*Ibid.*

[3]p. 259.

[4]*Ibid.*

[5]*Ibid.*

[6]p. 276.

[7]*Ibid.*

[8]p. 277.

[9]p. 273.

[10]p. 297.

[11]p. 261.

[12]p. 277.

[13]p. 264.

[14]Linda W. Wagner, *Dos Passos: Artist As American* (Austin: University of Texas Press, 1979), p. 47.

[15]John Dos Passos, *Manhattan Transfer* (1925; rpt. Boston: Houghton Mifflin Company, 1953), p. 217; henceforth all future references to this book will be followed with the page number(s).

[16]Townsend Ludington, *John Dos Passos: A Twentieth-Century Odyssey* (New York: E.P. Dutton, 1980), pp. 200-1.

CHAPTER IV

The City of Despair: Thomas Wolfe's *Of Time and the River* Nathanael West's *Miss Lonelyhearts*

New York City changed during the Great Depression of the 1930's. Like the rest of the Nation, it was afflicted by the economic hard times, but, unlike the rest of the Nation, these hard times had a more searing and lasting effect. New York had been preeminently the epitome of the ebulence and the gaiety that had characterized the 1920's. The Depression ended all this. Gone were the businesses that kept the windows of skyscrapers ablaze late into the night. The windows now presented a gaunt and foreboding appearance as they looked out upon a city increasingly surrounded by Hoovervilles. A malaise penetrated its very essence, for the Depression was not simply a story of bank failures and bankrupt businesses. It was the tragedy of countless homeless men and women on breadlines, the tragedy of those who were out of work and those who feared they would soon be out of work, and the tragedy of those who took their lives because there was no one who cared about their condition. Yet, even now, it was possible to look upon the City and see a glimmer of hope, a promise of rejuvenation. Some saw an inherent vitality in the immigrant ghettoes—the faint spark of humanity as people banded together in times of crisis. Everyone, after all, was in the same dilemma. Also, Wall Street, while depressed, was still functioning. New York City retained its status as the economic capital of the Nation, and Mayor LaGuardia, despite his ungainly shortness and nasal pitched voice (contrasting sharply with the suaveness of the former Jimmy Walker), projected a feeling, along with the handicapped President in the White House, that the government cared about the common man even if no one else did. But the relief that came brought with it a specific problem: the basic dehumanization of man's altruistic drives. Communal charity, no matter how noble its motives, was no substitute for the intimate bond achieved between an individual giver and receiver. In fact, some envisioned the relief programs of the 1930's as tainted by the very grimness that had brought them into being. Thousands were saved, but at the expense of human compassion. Salvation became a matter of governmental laws and programs. But the suffering was so great that this concern bothered few.

Visually, the City had greatly changed. A visitor to New York in the mid-thirties was immediately startled by the empty look of the buildings of lower Manhattan. For many it seemed as though a creeping paralysis had afflicted the City; its wharves, stores, and skyscrapers had become "tombstones of capitalism . . . with windows."[1] Mary Agnes Hamilton, a distinguished English visitor, was shocked to find the recently completed Empire State Building unlit and unable to pay its taxes except by "collecting dollars from the sightseers who ascend to its eyrie for the stupendous view to be got thence. . . ." The Waldorf, she ruefully noted, "is in the hands of the receivers. Stories of failing banks, turned-in motorcars, despairing suicides, are dinned into one's ears. . . ."[2] In his notes on the City, Stephen Longstreet recalled the overall sense of decay, and how "Great weathered girders of unfinished luxury apartments and hotels bled rust along Central Park South."[3] Construction on buildings and bridges begun before the Depression now ceased, and so many manufacturing firms left or went bankrupt that the City had less plants in operation than at any time since 1899.

Even more unsettling was the rise in Hoovervilles within and around the City, filled with the destitute and desperate, "with cord-tied packs or bundles under their arms, others wearing broken shoes and worn jackets, with no shirt underneath."[4] Notorious slums like "Lung Block," infamous for its large number of tuberculin cases, grew and perpetuated their evil influence on generations of inhabitants. As late as 1938, 50% of the tenements condemned in 1885 as unfit for human habitation were still standing. Architects referred to the City's tenement history as "one of the most shameful of human records."[5]

The Depression further magnified the dismal condition of the slums by making more pronounced their contrast against the remaining affluent of midtown Manhattan. A British visitor to the

City observed that a traveller need only digress a few blocks from the great thoroughfares of Lexington or Sixth Avenues to encounter "the slums . . . yelling about you."[6] Another observer was shocked that one could pass from "the sumptuous to the sordid within a good deal less than five hundred yards."[7] Writers for the WPA-sponsored *New York Panorama* decried these conditions in their study on the City. "More than any other American city," they concluded, "New York pitches high against low, rich against poor, the elegant against the squalid. All occur juxtaposed, with scarcely a buffer and rarely a disguise."[8]

Such were the physical manifestations of the Depression on the City. A more subtle effect appeared as a social malaise. Life became grim, gray, and meaningless. Some observed a cynicism permeating each strata of society—from the poor to the rich. Breadlines became the symbol of the times with their "grey-faced, shambling men, standing about in serried rows and groups. . . ."[9] The unemployed lost their pride, then their hope, shuffling from one shelter to another, begging for food, lining up outside missions for a free meal. In the Times Square area, theatre-goers were frequently jolted from their illusions by the rows of "shabby, utterly dumb and apathetic-looking men" waiting for the arrival of the coffee wagon run by W.R. Hearst of the *New York American*.[10] Stories abounded of people trying to cope: a young Ph.D. camping for eight months in Morningside Park, another soul loading all his possessions into a baby buggy. Some gave up the struggle and committed suicide. One joke had a hotel clerk asking guests if they wanted a room for sleeping or jumping. Some 1,595 New Yorkers killed themselves in 1932 alone—the highest number since 1900. There were also numerous reports of people starving. In 1931, New York hospitals recorded ninety-five deaths from starvation. Groucho Marx quipped that the times were so bad the pigeons had started to feed the people. New York City was no longer the city of dreams.

In the new environment, life became a perpetual struggle. People even had to work hard at having fun. Polly Adler's bordello, the most famous in town, lost its gaiety as clients, she noted, came more to drown their sorrows in liquor than sex. One client kept muttering that he used to control Wall Street but now did not have enough money to pay his rent. Another said he came there because it was the only place in town where he could cry without shame.

Broadway and its inhabitants began to exhibit a tawdriness in the eyes of some visitors. A writer for the London *Daily Express* likened the area to a "chorus girl who went to bed with her make-up on. . . . There is a cheapness and vulgarity everywhere, all masquerading under Broadway's favorite word, showmanship."[11] The former splendor had turned into "an angry carbuncle" on the face of a depressed city.[12]

Some observers of the City during the 1930's also noted an increase in the scope and viciousness of organized crime. With the passing of Prohibition, mobsters spread their influence into such areas as restaurants, theatres, bakeries, the garment trade, loansharking, prostitution, drugs, and gambling. Honest businessmen had to pay "protection" money or face a roughing up and a shattered shop. Politicians were frequently bribed, and New Yorkers grew hardened to the reports of Tamminy kickbacks, relatives on City payrolls, graft, and police corruption. For awhile it seemed as though criminals controlled the town. Few arrested in gambling raids were actually convicted. Of 514 arrests over a two-year period, only five cases arrived at court. As a Bronx political leader noted, letting people break the law now and then was the best way to garner votes at election time.

Yet underneath the ugliness a beauty remained. While the City had lost much of its splendor, it was still uniquely alive. Some observers found this vitality in the City's immigrant diversity, and marvelled how each enclave was impregnated by the national character. Europeans were especially delighted by the ability to "dine, drink, and amuse oneself on three continents."[13] Particularly exciting was the babble of languages heard on the streets. A Frenchwoman marvelled: "You cannot realize, on Broadway, that you are in America. This is the rendezvous of an international populo, especially on a Saturday evening. . . . The language you overhear isn't English either: Irish, German, Russian, Italian, Greek, Scandinavian, Jewish, all the accents, rolling, slurring, gargling, high-pitched, gutteral, clipped, mangle and murder the Anglo-Saxon idiom. . . ."[14] An early study by the WPA commented further on the complex intermingling of dialect and City environment: "Product of scores of nationalities, thousands of occupations and millions of people in necessary and constant contact, of whom some never leave the city while others come and go in a day, the New York language reflects every facet of a multifarious environment: the clatter of riveting guns, the sighs of the weary, the shrill warnings of policemen's whistles, the sunny chatter of perambulating nursemaids, the jittery laconisms of waiters, countermen, cabbies, musicians, busboys on the run, doctors, lawyers, nurses, thieves and radio entertainers."[15]

The City's vitality was evident in other areas too. One common trait shared by both the working and the unemployed was the need for cheap transportation. Mass transit expanded and improved during the mid- to late-1930's due to the combined efforts of Mayor LaGuardia and the Federal WPA Program. By the mid-thirties it was estimated that commuter passenger traffic entering the City averaged 300,000,000 annually. Over three billion passengers used the combined City transit, approximately sixty percent handled by the subway and elevated lines alone—figures truly astonishing when one remembers that the City was in the depths of a depression! Subway lines were expanded, and bridges and tunnels built to accommodate this increased volume of traffic. By the late thirties, over sixty bridges and sixteen tunnels connected Manhattan with the other Boroughs and New Jersey. One of the most spectacular achievements of this era, the George Washington Bridge, built in 1931 at a cost of $60,000,000, was the largest suspension bridge in the world at the time of completion. Its four roadway lanes and two pedestrian sidewalks spanned 3,500 feet over the Hudson River.

Growth could also be seen in the City's "vertical landscape." The Empire State Building was completed, rising 102 stories above midtown Manhattan, the tallest building in the world. The architect LeCorbusier envisioned the newly created RCA Building at Rockefeller Center as possessing a "mystical purity," projecting a vision of a new city, "a new event in human history which up to now had only a legend on that theme: that of the Tower of Babel."[16]

Such growth, however, was the end result of desperately needed relief. Between 1933 and 1939, New York received more than one billion dollars in aid from the Federal Government. During the peak year of 1936, nearly twenty percent of the City's entire population was on some form of public assistance, and much of the assistance came in the form of public works jobs intended to make the City a more beautiful place. Streets were improved; neighborhood renovations of housing projects, parks, and playgrounds were started; bridges and express highways were completed to relieve traffic congestion. Such activity, concluded LeCorbusier, clearly indicated that the City was not decaying but rather "in the process of becoming. . . . Crown of noble cities, soft pearls, or glittering topazes, or radiant lapis, or melancholy amethysts! New York is a great diamond, hard and dry, sparkling triumphant. . . ."[17]

Such jobs helped relieve the financial exigencies of the poor, but could not expunge the pain and humiliation many felt. Even if a man had a job and was able to feed his family, he frequently still labored under a burden of shame, largely self-imposed, for having been a failure. Men needed moral as well as financial assistance, and for many it came in the form of a new Mayor—Fiorello LaGuardia.

LaGuardia, unlike his dapper predecessor, Jimmy Walker, looked like anyone but a mayor. Short and plump with a high-pitched voice and a penchant for chasing fire engines and reading comic strips over the radio, he might in an earlier age have been viewed as totally unsuitable for the office. But in the 1930's, he represented, as did Roosevelt, the ability of one to overcome adversity and achieve great things. In short, his avant garde appearance and habits gave hope to the average man on the street. LaGuardia was a fighter, and as such, he viewed the City as a city under seige. He devoted much of his administration toward the creation of a new city—not simply a rebuilt one. For him, New York was to become "new . . . beautiful, healthful, and convenient; a more comfortable place in which to live, work, and play."[18] Toward these ends he labored and succeeded, for by the late 1940's, the French novelist, Simone deBeauvoir, found the City significantly if not disarmingly humane "as to belie its reputation for being hard and cold."[19]

LaGuardia's reforms were manifold. The unrestrained political corruption of the Walker years came under attack, as did police corruption. Organized crime was investigated for the first time, and the revelations were shocking. The eastern division of the national syndicate was headquartered in New York City and tightly run. Frank Costello was in charge of gambling; Lucky Luciano headed the prostitution and narcotics rackets; Dutch Schultz controlled the restaurants; Joseph Doto dominated the bail bond extortions and the Brooklyn waterfront; Louis "Lepke" Buchalter and Jacob "Gurrah" Shapiro ruled the industrial and labor extortions; and Benjamin "Bugsy" Siegel and Meyer Lansky were strong-arm enforces. LaGuardia's task was ominous!

Visitors to the City noted other effects of the LaGuardia administration. One praised its support of cultural and recreational outlets and saw in the making a "model city even from the social point of view."[20] Financial assistance was extended to include those not entirely, or even chiefly, victims of economic conditions. In 1938, 48,500 were old-age recipients, 1,300 blind, 13,000 homeless, 60,500 children in institutions, foster homes, or of poor parents, and 7,000 boys in CCC camps. During the LaGuardia years the City, for many, became a friendlier place. People knew that their government cared about them and they, in turn, became more caring themselves. Some visitors to New York at this time applauded the "readier adjustment and more harmony and mutual respect among the city's ethnic and racial groups, generally, than had been the case earlier in the century."[21]

Yet, despite the altruism and seemingly beneficial effects of relief, there lingered a nagging undercurrent of doubt as to its long-range effect. A product of government rather than of individuals, the "new" charity separated the giver from the receiver within a massive governmental bureaucracy. Relief became as impersonal as the City itself. It was standardized to the popular taste and reduced "to the zero level of value."[22] The new housing developments that replaced the squalid tenements of an earlier age dwarfed their inhabitants and fostered in many a desire to "punch a hole in every damned high building in every damned narrow street" to "let in the space, light and sky."[23] Reforms had been made but not without a cost, a cost inevitable in an ever-expanding city on the perimeter of a new era.

When *Of Time and the River* appeared in 1935, Thomas Wolfe was at the peak of his literary career. His rise to fame had been nothing less than spectacular. American and foreign critics had extravagantly praised his first novel, *Look Homeward Angel* (1929), and Sinclair Lewis even went so far as to declare the young author as "one of the greatest world writers."[24] This was truly an auspicious beginning for Wolfe, but the royalties were nevertheless small—even by the standards of the day—and he frequently found himself short of cash and reluctantly begging financial assistance from his editor, Maxwell Perkins, at Scribner's. Unlike some of the successful writers of his time, Wolfe could never divorce himself completely from the economic exigencies of the Depression. But even if he could have, it is doubtful that he would have because of his moral conscience. This conscience is evident throughout his second work, *Of Time and the River*, and especially in the section "Proteus: the City."

"Proteus," like the novel, deals with the life of Eugene Gant during the early 1920's. But the action and events are so reflective of Wolfe's own experiences, doubts, and questionings throughout the thirties that it can easily be classified as a period piece of the new decade. Deeply affected by the Depression, Wolfe noted in *The Story of a Novel* how the events of those years had "soaked in on him" during his nocturnal wanderings within the City:

> In this endless quest and prowling of the night through the great web and jungle of the city, I . . . felt . . . the full weight of that horrible human calamity. . . . And the staggering impact of this black picture of man's inhumanity to his fellow man, the unending repercussions of these scenes of suffering, violence, oppression, hunger, cold, and filth and poverty going on unheeded in a world in which the rich were still rotten with their wealth left a scar upon my life, a conviction in my soul which I shall never lose.[25]

When similar sentiments were projected upon Gant, Perkins objected, insisting that Gant remain "colored a good deal by the romantic aestheticism" of the previous decade. "Old Tom has been trying to change his book into some kind of Marxian argument . . ." he complained to Hemingway.[26] Evidently, a compromise was reached. Wolfe could express his opinions but only obliquely, through implication. Perkins realized that it would have been unfair, if not impossible, for the author to totally dismiss the Depression from the novel, and nowhere do these feelings of the times appear more vividly than in "Proteus: the City."

The tone of this section, however, is also reflective of the personal anxiety Wolfe suffered prior to the completion of the novel. Richard Kennedy has noted that during these years Wolfe's personal life was about as turbulent and as tragic as the economic crisis at hand: "Wolfe had not been unhappier and more unhinged than at any other time of his life. Entries in his pocket notebook . . . show the unhealthy state of mind that produced *Death the Proud Brother* and 'A Vision of Death in April.' Lists in May and June contain dark subjects for his writing: deaths, symptoms of madness, details of burning jealousy in love, situations of shame . . ., incidents of fear, examples of hatred and loathing, nightmares. . . ."[27]

Bothered by Scribner's deadlines, Wolfe worked long hours and could not sleep from anxiety. He lost weight, felt exhausted, and was frequently irritable. After returning from a few days' trip to Vermont with a friend, he wrote to his mother: "I was exhausted, and could go no further—had an attack of ptomaine poisoning and sheer nervous fatigue—cramps in stomach and unable to hold food—so had to get away."[28] One passage from his notebook that captures the tone of the "Proteus" section as well as his thoughts of the Great Depression is entered on January 1, 1932:

> Yesterday was the last day of one of the unhappiest, dreariest years in the nation's history. The depression, so-called, has a strong and oppressive physical quality. Just how one feels this I don't know, but we breathe it in the air, and we get it in a harassed and weary feeling which people have: the terrible thing in America now, however, is not the material bankruptcy but the spiritual one. Instead of revolution—which is a coherent and living act of the spirit—one feels the presence of something worse—a mindless chaos, and millions of people blundering about without a belief in anything, without hope, with apathy and cynicism. We seem to be lost. The faces of the people in the subway are sometimes horrible in their lack of sensitivity and intelligence—they ruminate mechanically at wads of gum, the skins are horrible blends of the sallow, the pustulate, the greasy: and the smell that comes from this is acrid, foul and weary. They are all going home into that immensity of mindless sprawling horror and ugliness which is known as Brooklyn.[29]

Similar dismal sentiments in "Proteus" did not go unnoticed by the critics who, while praising the entire novel's exuberant "belief in America," nevertheless saw in it a vivid "social document" of the times where the "present order is sterile of beauty and dignity, division between classes is sharp and inseparable, and in the last analysis man's great enemy is himself."[30]

This City of despair in "Proteus" is a projection of the senses and imagination of Eugene Gant. A pall of gloom permeates every dimension of New York and is magnified by his own negative outlook on life in which,

> the world swarmed blindly, nauseously, drunkenly about him. He looked at the faces in the hotel lobby, the brawling, furious, and

chaotic street, and the swarming and rancid corridors, with dizzy swimming eyes and a constricted heart; a thousand unutterable and horrible premonitions and imaginings of ruin and shame swarmed through his mind—every day he felt the impending menace of some new and fatal catastrophe, some indefinable and crushing disgrace with which each hour was ominously, murderously pregnant.[31]

This outlook is only relieved when Gant takes a brief trip up the Hudson River to visit a wealthy friend of his Harvard days. Temporarily hypnotized by the luxurious surroundings, he finds his new environment "beautiful and right and good." (p. 539) But in time, his perception of these surroundings also changes, and they become tainted by the cruelty and shallowness of the age.

Part of Gant's confused perception lies in his having Southern roots. When he arrives in the City, his rural, Southern naivete is immediately arrested by the City's high and magnificent dimensions. To him it is truly a Babylon on the Hudson, a city of enchantment:

He stared gape-mouthed, he listened, he saw the whole thing blazing in his face again to the tone and movement of its own central, unique, and incomparable energy. It was so real that it was magical, so real that all that men had always known was discovered to them instantly, so real he felt as if he had known it forever, yet must be dreaming as he looked at it; therefore he looked at it and his spirit cried:
    "Incredible! Oh, incredible! It moves, it pulses like a single living thing! It lives, it lives, with all its million faces"—and this is the way he always knew it was. (p. 419)

But this immediate response is not lasting. Once acclimated to his new environment, he discovers another New York, a depression New York, a New York of false promises and filled with petty, unsatisfied inhabitants who jostle each other,

like the embodiment of all the frustrate hunger, desire, and fury he had come to know in the city, with a terrible wordless evocation of men starving in the heart of a great plantation, of men dying of thirst within sight of a shining spring, with a damnable mockery, a nightmare vision of proud, potent and hermetic flesh, of voluptuous forms in hell, forever near, forever palpable, but never to be known, owned, or touched. (p. 479)

Concomitant with the frustration is the heartlessness of the concrete City, impervious and unfeeling toward the men who have created and inhabit it and who cry out:

> Gigantic city, we have taken nothing—not even a handful of your trampled dust—we have made no image on your iron breast and left not even the print of a heel upon your stony-hearted pavements. The possession of all things, even the air we breathed, was held from us, and the river of life and time flowed through the grasp of our hands forever, and we held nothing for our hunger and desire except the proud and trembling moments, one by one. (p. 509)

What particularly makes the City "stony-hearted" is that it is the antithesis of what is natural and essentially wholesome for man's development. While teaching at the university, Gant is daily offended and appalled by the "tiled sterility" of his hotel lobby, the "dusty beaten light and violence" of the street outside, and the "brawling and ugly corridors" of the university. Mankind is crushed within this environment and is reduced to a physical presence of unpleasant sensations such as the "hot and swarthy body-smells," the "strong female odors of rut and crotch and arm-pit and cheap perfume," and the male smells—"rancid, stale, and sour . . ." of the students. (pp. 419-420)

But the City assaults more than the senses; it assaults the individuality of man and attempts to reduce him to the will of the mob. Gant finds himself daily imprisoned by its "manswarm" devoid of the "essences of individual character and memory." (p. 423) Especially depressing are the gray felt hats worn by New Yorkers:

> they seemed to be the badge, the uniform, of a race of mechanical creatures, who were as essential and inhuman a part of the city's substance as stone and steel and brick, who had been made of one essential substance and charged with one general and basic energy along with the buildings, tunnels, streets, and a million glittering projectiles of machinery . . . the mindless and unwitting automatons of a gigantic and incomprehensible pattern. (p. 423)

In such a city the ideals of the artist, the creator, become "the deathless bird-song" sunken beneath the "furious glare and clamor of the city's life. . . ." (p. 425) The great plans of architects are no longer designs for the living but rather the barren and blind "proliferations of the manswarm . . . to shelter, house, turn out, take in, all the nameless, faceless, mindless manswarm atoms of the earth." (p. 429) The buildings of the university are devoid of the regenerative and creative spirit of knowledge. Instead, a "lifeless air" permeates the hallways and rooms, "the walls, the furniture, the floors—every part of the building—seemed to exude this sense of nervous depletion." (p. 442) Youth decays to a death-in-life condition where bitterness and violence predominate. In the street-wise youth of the City, Gant sees the,

> waning violence of the tenement, bitterly to try to root its meagre life into the rootless rock, meagrely to struggle in its infamous small phlegm along the pavements, feebly to imitate the feeble objects of its base idolatry—of which the most heroic was a gangster, the most sagacious was a pimp, the most witty was some Broadway clown. (pp. 498-499)

And in each instance the City stands apart from nature, apart and isolated by the river surrounding it, which for Gant becomes "unutterably the language of all he had ever thought or felt or known of America. . . ." (p. 569)

Within the river lies a vitality absent from the man-made City. It is a vitality born of Nature. New York offers a different vitality, a vitality that is ambiguously attractive yet unsettling, for it is "grimy and illimitable," reflective of a city structure, "smutted with the rust and grime of its vast works and factories," yet "indestructible and everlasting. . . ." (p. 571)

But this vitality can also become the vitality of violence, a brutal struggle for survival—devoid of reason and of love. In such a city, the faces of men are stamped "with all the familiar markings of suspicion and mistrust, cunning, contriving, and a hard and stupid cynicism." (p. 416) It has even perverted the faculty at the university:

> their flesh got green and yellow with its poisons, the air about them was webbed, cross-webbed, and counter-webbed with the dense fabric of their million spites and hatreds. They wasted and grew sick with hate and poison because another man received promotion, because another man had got his poem printed, because another man had eaten food and swallowed drink and lain with women, and lived and would not die; they sweltered with hate and fear. . . . (p. 421)

Out on the street a similar but more brutal drama is presented when Gant visits the brother of his friend and former student, Abe Jones, on the Lower East Side. As they walk down a dismal, deserted street by the waterfront, bottles begin to shatter around them, hurled by the hands of unseen local toughs. Gant learns from his friend that such incidents are common in a neighborhood noted for "one of the most criminal gangs." (p. 495) He also learns that Abe's brother has had to repeatedly ward off attacks from these gangs demanding "protection" money, and that much of the Jones' family's history is a litany of "bloody fights waged back and forth across these pavements. . . . Thus, in pier and alley, on street and roof, children had learned the arts of murder, the smell of blood, the odor of brains upon the pavement." (p. 496) The City has become the city of despair, and its vitality lies in its violence alone.

The humanity of man is lost somewhere on the outskirts of the City for it is here, as seen at the beginning of "Proteus," that the lethargy characteristic of New Yorkers is temporarily replaced with a feeling of healthy competition in which a subtle cord of humanity links all men and women. New Yorkers in "Proteus" are essentially an isolated and fearful people. But on the trains heading into the City, an incident occurs that lifts them out of their daydreams, worries, and preoccupations into a sense of sharing. The incident is the race between the train Gant is on "pounding North across New Jersey" and another bound from Philadelphia on an inside track. As the passengers on each train gradually become aware that a race is occurring, their mood changes:

> now the faces that had been so gray and dead were flushed with color, the dull and lustreless eyes had begun to burn with joy and interest. The passengers of both trains crowded to the windows, grinning like children for delight and jubilation. (p. 408)

But once the race is over and the trains near the City, the passengers return to their former joyless behavior reflecting the approaching environment:

> outside there was the raw and desolate-looking country, there were the great steel coaches, the terrific locomotives, the shining rails, the sweep of the tracks, the vast indifferent dinginess and rust of colors, the powerful mechanical expertness, and the huge indifference to suave finish. (p. 410)

The City's deadly grip is unavoidable.

It is this impersonality of the City and its inhabitants that reappears over and over in "Proteus" until it becomes the most characteristic trait of city life. For Wolfe, who like Gant, walked the nameless streets observing the countless, colorless, shuffling men outside the mission houses, waiting for a free meal or a place to sleep, it *was* the City. Furthermore, its permanence is due to the fact that it is primarily the creation of fear—the "fear" that President Roosevelt labelled the greatest obstacle faced by the people of the Depression. Fear dominates Eugene Gant's life and the lives of the people around him. It assumes the dimensions of a nightmare, a "gray lipless shape . . . legible in the faces, the movements, and the driven frenzied glances of the people who swarmed on the streets. What was this thing that duped men out of joy, tricked them out of all the exultant and triumphant music of the world, drove them at length into the dusty earth, cheated, defrauded, tricked out of life by a nameless phantom, with all their glory wasted?" (pp. 420-421)

Such fear destroys the intrinsic humanity of the city dweller. First, it isolates him from his fellow man. Gant's residence, the Leopold, has rooms described as "cells" which house not people but the bitter remnants of a defeated society, "museum relics of what had once been a family rather than . . . the living and organic reality." (p. 430) And second, it produces a "feeling of naked insecurity, a terrifying transciency . . . the horrible transciency of lives held here for a period in the illusion of a brief and barren permanence, of lives either on the wing or on the wane." (p. 430) Gone is the exuberance of the twenties, and in its place lies the stiffling pangs of "hope, hunger, passion, bitter lonliness and earth-devouring fury. . . ." (p. 430) In short, the Leopold is a reflection of a city and a nation without a future.

This malaise infects the students at the university, victims of "the wordless horror of this damned and blasted waste of Dead-Man's Land, (with its) . . . futility and desolation." (p. 464) It subverts friendship and the love between men and women. Letters become exchanges of "personal insult and invective, the desire to crow over the other man and humiliate him. . . ." (p. 465); and intimacy is reduced to a diseased, adulterous, and verbally abusive affair as is witnessed in the relationship between two of Gant's friends, Robert and Martha.

Human relationships are also chaotic because men and women are defective within themselves. For Wolfe, the City absorbs its citizens, leaving behind mere shells of former humanity. The outlines of the human physique are chiselled into hard angularity by the City's heartlessness. Abe Jones represents such a figure, and his surface ugliness has mistakenly led some to criticize Wolfe for being anti-Semitic. Jones' "dull, and slanting forehead, almost reptilian in its ugliness" is not a comment on his race but upon a body, twisted and shaped over the years by the mean streets of the Lower East Side:

> He was about the middle height, and neither thin nor fat: his figure was rather big-boned and angular, and yet it gave an impression of meagreness, spareness, and somewhat tallowy toughness which so many city people have, as if their ten thousand days and nights upon the rootless pavement had dried all juice and succulence out of them, as if asphalt and brick and steel had got into the conduits of their blood and spirit, leaving them with a quality that is tough, dry, meagre, tallowy, and somewhat calloused. (pp. 457-458)

His sister, Sylvia, also possesses the hard angularity of city life as well as the added dimension of its artificial glitter:

> There was a remarkably . . . unnaturalness about her: it seemed as if the only light that had ever shone upon her had been electric light, the only air she could breath with any certitude and joy, the clamorous and electric air of Broadway. (p. 459)

Like her brother, she too mirrors the "furious and feverish" life of the City, and her flesh is starved and wasted by the unrest and discontent around her.

Thus Abe and his sister are the end result of the City and its cruelty. For the most part, they, and all New Yorkers, have withdrawn into an insulated consciousness immune to the suffering around them. Preeminent in survival are the New York Jews:

> incorrupt, old and cautious, filled with skill and safety—that they had lived so long and grown so wise and crafty that their subtile, million-noted minds could do without and hold in dark contempt the clumsy imperfections of a fleshly evil—that they could evoke and live completely in a world of cruel and subtle intuitions, unphrased and unutterable intensities of cruelty, shame, and horror, without lifting a finger or turning a hand. (p. 481)

It is survival, but survival at a price, for it forsakes humanity and withdraws from the active world which forever remains "phantom and remote." (p. 494) It is the existence of a self-imposed prisoner, limited by the restraints of ignorance and fear, and in such an existence life is always untested, untried, and unlived.

In a city where isolation is a prerequisite for survival, meaningful communication must cease. In "Proteus," the characters are stranded—intentionally or unintentionally—within the hectic pace of the City. Any attempt to bridge the gap between individuals is either aborted or halfheartedly achieved. Gant's female students simultaneously seduce and reject him. They become erotic temptresses "receiving, giving, returning and withdrawing" their attentions. (pp. 478-479) The mournful Jews of the Lower East Side, isolated from the mainstream of city life either due to prejudice or their own choice, maintain their lives confined to the borders of their ghetto world, walking between shops and homes, engaging in blind strivings for culture and beauty. Gant envisions them,

> returning through a thousand streets, in that waning and desolate light, from symphony concerts, an image, which, so far from giving a note of hope, life, and passionate certitude and joy to the wordless horror of this damned and blasted waste of Dead-Man's Land, seemed to enhance it rather, and to give it a conclusive note of futility and desolation. (p. 464)

One of Gant's friends, Robert, is driven by a bitter, desperate, and suicidal lonliness masked by an effusive friendliness. An "outcast of orderly society," he sets his room on fire at the Leopold, yet begs not to be turned out. He is a man who simultaneously accepts and rejects the world around him in a frenzy of paranoid schizophrenia. Returning from a Western trip, he appears to Gant to be wasted in body and spirit:

> He no longer cared whether he lived or died, in his inmost heart he had grown amorous of death, and it was evident that living flesh and bone could not much longer endure the cruel beating he had given it. And this fact—this shocking, visible, physical fact—as much as anything—sealed him in fatal desperation, confirmed him in his belief that everything was lost. (p. 454)

In the end, the City, like Robert, becomes diseased with its citizens paradoxically a part of, yet isolated from, the lives of their fellow citizens. Communication degenerates into the curiosity of slander filled with a "corrupt and venomous joy" that seizes on every story of man's "dishonor, defeat, or sorrow" and greets any evidence of compassion or love with a vicious sneer. (pp. 421-422)

Gant briefly escapes from this dismal world when he visits a wealthy friend of his Harvard days, Joel Pierce, whose family owns a venerable mansion on the banks of the upper Hudson River. On the surface they represent a world of beauty and refinement that lifts the soul above the rottenness and decay of New York City. It is here, Gant initially believes, that the restorative power in Nature ennobles man and bestows on him a virtuousness:

> It was not merely the wealth, the luxury and the comfort of the scene that filled his heart with a sense of joy and victory. Far more than this, it was the feeling that this life of wealth, and luxury and comfort was so beautiful and right and good. At the moment it seemed to him to be the life for which all men on the earth are seeking, about which all men living dream, toward which all the myriads of the earth aspire; and the thing, above all, which made this life seem so beautiful and good was the conviction that filled him at that moment of its essential incorruptible righteousness. (p. 539)

Such a world, Gant is certain, possesses standards by which all men can live. But his perception is again naive; for even this world he admires has a strained, artificial quality about it that taints everything it touches. It is a truth that lurks on the borders of Gant's mind and occasionally breaks through his ecstatic reveries.

The first indication of his growing awareness occurs when he attends a Broadway show with Joel and Mr. Pierce. The audience in the playhouse is largely composed of the elegant set, and the play is apparently a work that is geared for their style and taste. As it proceeds from scene to scene, Gant is shocked by a certain air of artificiality in the audience's response to the play. There is a distinctive hollowness in their laughter which is "somewhat strained and metallic." (p. 503) It reflects the falseness of these people as well as the show, an example of, "a new and disagreeable mirth . . . coming into man's life, which seemed to have its sources not in the warm human earth and blood of humor, but to proceed from something sterile, sour and acrid. . . ." (p. 503) The laughter is not founded on sincerity or any sympathy for the play or the lives it represents. Instead it is the polite and refined laughter of a soulless people who need a diversion from their own "nakedness and insecurity." (p. 503)

This audience serves as the archetype of the Pierce clan and their friends along the upper Hudson Valley. They, too, are insecure. Joel's winning smile and manners become standardized and repetitious, and Gant's initial admiration becomes confused by the obvious moral decay present. Upon arriving at the estate, he is treated with hospitality but soon encounters circles of vicious gossip similar to that found in the City. The only person who seems to rise above this level is George Thorton, but his withdrawal is due to a creeping insanity, "a man whose extreme reasonableness comes from a fear of madness, whose temperance from some fatal impulse to insane excess." (p. 518)

Gant's confusion then suddenly evolves into a rage as he realizes "how men had groped and toiled and mined, and grown blind and bent and gray, deep in the dark bowels of the earth, to wreak this moonlight loveliness upon a hill . . . how men had sweat and women worked, how youth had struck its fire and grown old, how hope and faith and even love had died, how many nameless lives had labored, grieved, and come to naught in order that this fragile image of compacted night, this priceless distillation of its rare and chosen loveliness, should blossom to a flower of moonlight beauty on a hill." (pp. 539-540)

This insight places every other aspect of the Hudson Valley rich into focus. Their artificiality, coldness, arrogance, vanity, and falseness stem from an insensitive lifestyle. The Pierce library includes a collection of the "great poets of the earth," but the volumes lie, "unread, unopened, and forgotten," the "mute small symbols of a rich man's power, of the power of wealth to own everything." (p. 589) The library represents wealth without knowledge—a world where the value of things is determined more by their visual effect than their merit.

The visual predominates in all things. Miss Felfair, a friend and neighbor, is described as a piece of art with "nail-bevarnished hand, a few crisp words of greeting, and a quick light smile, as brittle, frail, and painted as a bit of china." (p. 573) The automobiles at the train station are lines up with a "stamped-out quality, a kind of metallic and inhuman repetition." (p. 593) Gant sees in the faces of their owners a similar quality. It is the spirit of the Depression, a desperation tempered with callosed numbness, where "life and lustre and fire of youth" have vanished forever. (p. 593) Mrs. Pierce and her stepmother are vain, conceited women whose sole preoccupation is "keeping fit." (p. 554) The younger maintains a "stern regimen, grim watchfulness, and unflagging effort," while the older can only ape the "airs and manners of a coquette" in her effort to "enslave every man she met under the domination of her captivating charm." (p. 560) In dealing with these women, Gant is numbed by a soul-chilling coldness of spirit. Neither possesses any understanding or concern for humanity. When he attempts to explain his midnight wanderings to Mrs. Pierce, he finds himself stricken dumb and senseless, frozen by "the proud and haughty magnificence of her person," and her "inhuman detachment." (pp. 532, 534)

Even his friend, Joel, marks himself by advising Gant to put on a coat whenever walking past the grandfather's house. The innocuous statement caps Gant's awareness that "the enchanted world of wealth and love and beauty, of living fulfillment and of fruitful power, which he had visioned as a child in all his dreams about the fabled rich along the Hudson River—did not exist." (p. 570) Neither in the center of the City or along the upper Hudson Valley is there any relief for the oppressed senses of Eugene Gant, and on the train going home to the Leopold he sees the final statement of a city's despair and a nation's lost vision in the "idiot profanity" of a frenzied alcoholic.

Like Wolfe, Nathanael West found himself "infected" with the Depression. But for West the infection was more deeply rooted in the subconscious, since his whole life reflected those times. If the 1930's crystallized the spiritual, social, and economic decay of a nation and its people, West's own life can be considered a condensed reflection of the agony and the shame that would find its fullest expression in *Miss Lonelyhearts*.

A brief look at West's life reveals a foundation of experiences upon which his novel would be built. As the only son of Lithuanian Jewish immigrants, he had a painfully self-conscious and anxious childhood that would later result in his changing his name from Weinstein to the Anglicized West, and his habitual avoidance of most Jewish religious, cultural, and social associations.

Without a firm identity or confident self-image, West opted for a pessimistic, iconoclastic world-view that greatly influenced his art.

Dropping out of high school, he forged a transcript to gain admittance to Tufts College, dropped out during the first term, and during the following term again used falsified records to gain admittance to Brown University, from which he eventually graduated in 1924. Ironically, such deception was not necessary, for West had the ability to easily handle the scholastic world. He did well in the courses he enjoyed (English and Art). He had many out-of-class interests such as modernist literature and modern art, and he published in the college literary magazine. While at Brown he also became the center of a small group of aspiring writers, among whom was S.J. Perelman, a life-long friend and future brother-in-law. West's diffident attitude toward his studies and academia in general were therefore not reflective of any dullness on his part, but rather a flippancy toward all the trappings of the established contemporary culture he simultaneously wooed and rejected.

West's dissatisfaction and iconoclasm intensified as he grew older. By the early 1930's, he found himself consciously committed to a writing career but still at considerably loose ends with himself. Nathan Asch remembered him at this time as a "sophisticated, ironic personality." He "looked as I suppose Michael Arlen would have liked to look," and he talked "as if he didn't actually believe that what was happening around him was really happening and he didn't much like it anyway."[32]

This, however, was merely a pose masking a sensitive nature both at odds with, yet fascinated by, the increasingly dismal world of the Depression. While not rich, West never suffered extreme poverty during the 1930's. An uncle set him up as a night manager in a Manhattan hotel. And he later made a handsome income as a Hollywood scriptwriter for modest "B" films. This nevertheless did not lessen the spiritual malaise of the Depression that was recorded every day in his life. While working at the Kenmore & Sutton Hotels in New York City, he was exposed to a more dismal side of the Depression. Many of the patrons were down on their luck, and the sundeck at the Sutton gained a dubious distinction as "Suicide's Leap." Friends of West recalled that years after his leaving the hotel work for Hollywood, he remained fascinated and appalled by his recollections of those desperate and hopeless lives.

Also while working at the Sutton, West was exposed to another world that would contribute to *Miss Lonelyhearts*; this was the Bohemian world of Greenwich Village. Everything about the Village and its denizens appealed to West's iconoclastic nature. Here there were, at least, no sacred cows except in not having any sacred cows. The political environment was radical, and West participated in "Popular Front" activities. He also met a wide variety of people from all walks of life and professions. One, a columnist who wrote under the pseudonym of "Susan Chester" for the *Brooklyn Eagle*, supplied him with examples of letters she received as editor of the lovelorn column. West saw in the unintentional pathos and tragedy of the letters, signed with such names as "Broad Shoulders," the suffering of a nameless race of city dwellers that would reappear in *Miss Lonelyhearts*. Finally, West's exposure to the literary circles of the Village and their emphasis on Surrealism, satire, and symbol further developed his taste for the absurd. Besides imbibing the Dada-Surrealist sensibility found in the "little magazines," he worked briefly as an associate editor of the *Americana*, a satirical magazine. Under these influences, West's literary outlook took on a decidedly nihilistic tone of distorted perceptions where a man's cheeks would be described as rolls of toilet paper or a woman's buttocks as enormous grindstones. For West, even the novel's form had to transcend the conventions of the rational, for what was rational in the 1930's with the world in collapse? Thus *Miss Lonelyhearts* was intended, as one critic has noted, "in the form of a comic strip. The chapters to be squares in which many things happen through one action. . . . Each chapter instead of going forward in time, also goes backward, forward, up and down in space like a picture."[33]

Such stylistic bizarreness in *Miss Lonelyhearts* dumbfounded the critics, but convinced them that in West's bitter rendition of New York could be seen the quintessential mood of the Depression, a mood that paralyzed the Nation as well as the City. One critic, Josephine Herbst, perceptively noted this when she wrote: "The entire jumble of modern society, bankrupt not only in cash but more tragically in emotion, is depicted here like a life-sized engraving narrowed down to the head of a pin."[34]

The City as depression in microcosm is certainly the New York of *Miss Lonelyhearts*. Like the dead City of Eugene Gant in *Of Time and the River*, the New York of Miss Lonelyhearts, heartache columnist for the New York *Post-Dispatch*, is a dismal landscape without relief. As a columnist, he responds to the pathetic letters of people on the verge of suicide—to people who no longer have hope or for whom hope is vain in a society that refuses to recognize their dreams. While dining at El Gaucho, he encounters people who, like his readers, are entrapped by futile ambitions:

> He had learned not to laugh at the advertisements offering to teach writing, cartooning, engineering, to add inches to the biceps and to develop the bust. He should therefore realize that the people who came to El Gaucho were the same as those who wanted to write and live the life of an artist, wanted to be an engineer and wear leather puttees, wanted to develop a grip that would impress the boss, wanted to cushion Raoul's head on their swollen breasts. They were the same people as those who wrote to Miss Lonelyhearts for help.[35]

Hollywood is largely responsible for this situation because it has generated false beliefs perpetuated by "the movies, radio and newspapers." "Among many betrayals," Miss Lonelyhearts concludes, "this one is the worst," for it plays upon the imagination of men seeking salvation from the brutal reality of their existence:

> He saw a man who appeared to be on the verge of death stagger into a movie theater that was showing a picture called *Blonde Beauty*. He saw a ragged woman with an enormous goiter pick a love story magazine out of a garbage can and seem very excited by her find. (p. 39)

The personal dilemma of Miss Lonelyhearts, however, evolves primarily from his capacity for "dreaming the Christ dream." In his dream, he becomes the principal idealist in a city without ideals, which in turn paralyzes his aspirations. His attempts to relieve the suffering of his correspondents is reduced to stock clichés ("Christ died for you. . . . Cherish this gift. . . .") (p. 39), and the concomitant realization that all relief is useless:

> He snatched the paper out of the machine. With him, even the word Christ was a vanity. After staring at the pile of letters on his desk for a long time, he looked out the window. A slow spring rain was changing the dusty tar roofs below him to shiny patent leather. The water made everything slippery and he could find no support for either his eyes or his feelings. (p. 39)

As such, his failure to live the Christ dream lies not, as he believes, in his lack of humility, but rather in his failure to completely empathize with the suffering around him. Suffering, after all, is the norm in Miss Lonelyhearts' city, and he has become immune to it like everyone else.

Consequently, he serves as the chief exponent of the City's personality—paralyzed and cold at the soul, possessing little, if any, sympathy. Sitting at his desk at the newspaper, he finds himself becoming inured to the countless tales of human misery and suffering that pass through his hands each day. For him the "city room" is a "desert . . . not of sand, but of rust and body dirt, surrounded by a book-yard fence on which are posters describing the events of the day. Mother slays five with ax, slays seven, slays nine. . . ." (pp. 24-25) The people of the City are the nameless "Desperate" and "Broken-hearted," and Lonelyhearts' commiseration assumes the artificial cooing of a third-rate sermon nobody can believe:

> "Life, for most of us, seems a terrible struggle of pain and heart-break, without hope or joy. Oh, my dear readers, it only seems so. Every man, no matter how poor or humble, can teach himself to use his senses. See the cloud-flecked sky, the foam-decked sea. . . . Smell the sweet pine and heady privet. . . . Feel of velvet and of satin. . . . As the popular song goes, 'the best things in life are free'." (p. 26)

In his heart, he searches for but fails to find the true answers needed to genuinely help his correspondents, and being only human and vulnerable, he assumes the callousness of a rock, "a solidification of his feeling, his conscience, his sense of reality, his self knowledge." (p. 56)

Alongside the death of feeling and emotion is the growing mechanization and standardization of city life. All around Miss Lonelyhearts a mechanized sterility subverts every aspect of man's environment. Even the restorative influence of Nature has been reduced to a mechanized grimness that makes it more oppressive than beneficial. The air smells as though it has been artificially heated. A walk through the park fails to reveal any signs of Spring:

> The decay that covered the surface of the mottled ground was not the kind in which life generates. Last year, he remembered, May had failed to quicken these soiled fields. It had taken all the brutality of July to torture a few green spikes through the exhausted dirt. (pp. 4-5)

There is no Spring in Miss Lonelyhearts' soul either, and his attempts at stimulation ("hot water, whiskey, coffee, exercise, and sex") leave him cold and uninspired: "Like a dead man, only friction could make him warm or violence make him mobile." (p. 19) Trying to break free from his predicament, he finds himself forever being thrown back upon the sterile contours of the City. The skyscrapers with their "tons of forced rock and tortured steel" menace the small deserted parks he frequents, and even the shadows around him become distorted, lengthened jerks against a swollen and dying sun. (p. 19) Harmony tends toward disharmony in his world where every "order has within it the germ of destruction." (p. 31) On a trip to the Connecticut woods, he finds no relief for his withered viewpoint. Lurking in the shades are the ever-present symbols of decay and disillusionment, "nothing but death—rotten leaves, gray and white fungi, and over everything a funereal hush." (p. 38)

Consequently, the traditional roles of love and family as restoratives and stability hold forth little promise in Miss Lonelyhearts' world. Love and sex in the novel frequently assume an unhealthy, sadistic aggressiveness, as when some of Miss Lonelyhearts' male friends conclude at the bar of a speakeasy that the best way to control women with literary or intellectual pretentiousness is with a "good rape." (p. 14) In the midst of such talk, Lonelyhearts becomes aware of their inherent childishness, their impotent fury directed against women, not as fellow humans but rather as objects that threaten their only remaining source of identity—their masculinity:

> At college, and perhaps for a year afterwards, they had believed in literature, had believed in Beauty and in personal expression as an absolute end. When they lost this belief, they lost everything. Money and fame meant nothing to them. They were not worldly men. (p. 14)

Miss Lonelyhearts is not immune to this pervasive sterility of feeling that afflicts his friends, for he too finds himself incapable of loving or being loved. None of his relationships with women approaches a level of intimacy that indicates a deep sympathy. His adulterous affair with Fay Doyle is likened to a tedious swim on a strong sea: "Her call for him to hurry was a sea-moan, and when he lay beside her, she heaved, tidal, moondriven." (p. 28) If anything, she is symbolic of the primal, procreative urge of Nature, but the drives leave Miss Lonelyhearts exhausted like "a swimmer leaving the surf. . . ." (p. 28) A similarly adulterous affair with Mary Shrike is equally unsatisfying. Her frigidity and incessant preoccupation with her mother's death from breast cancer keep him, as well as her husband, at a distance. Miss Lonelyhearts thinks of her as the Virgin Mary.

His conclusion about Mary is another indication of his serious dilemma, since religion is his ultimate hope for redemption from his own problems as well as those of his readers. But the "Christ dream," like Mary's love, is soured and impotent. It takes on the rote doggeral of Shrike's mocking prayer:

"Soul of Miss L, glorify me.
Body of Miss L, nourish me.
Blood of Miss L, intoxicate me.
Tears of Miss L, wash me.
Oh good Miss L, excuse my plea.
And hide me in your heart,
And defend me from mine enemies.
Help me, Miss L, help me, help me.
In saecula saeculorum. Amen." (p. 1)

His faith eventually degenerates into a sort of fanaticism while he assumes the posture of a rock "calm and solid," able to "withstand any test . . ." (p. 52), conversing with God:

He was conscious of two rhythms that were slowly becoming one. When they became one, his identification with God was complete. His heart was the one heart, the heart of God. And his brain was likewise God's. (p. 57)

Miss Lonelyhearts' religion has become as destructively mechanized as everyone and everything in the novel. Nor is his faith unique, as one newspaper headline testifies:

"ADDING MACHINE USED IN RITUAL OF WESTERN SECT . . .
Figures Will Be Used for Prayers for Condemned Slayer of Aged Recluse . . . DENVER, COLO., Feb. 2 (A.P.) Frank H. Rice, Supreme Pontiff of the Liberal Church of America, has announced he will carry out his plan for a 'goat and adding machine' ritual for William Moya, condemned slayer, despite objection to his program by a Cardinal of the sect. Rice declared the goat would be used as part of a

sack cloth and ashes' service shortly before and after Moya's execution, set for the week of June 20. Prayers for the condemned man's soul will be offered on an adding machine. Numbers, he explained, constitute the only universal language. Moya killed Joseph Zemp, an aged recluse, in an argument over a small amount of money." (p. 7)

With such religions, humanism is suffocated—the very humanism essential for religion to be restorative. There is no longer the inspiration of great deeds: "the sky holds no angels, flaming crosses, olive-bearing doves, wheels within wheels. Only a newspaper struggled in the air like a kite with a broken spine." (p. 5) The stirrings in Miss Lonelyhearts' soul as a youth in his father's church, the discovery that something special stirred in him when he shouted the name of Christ, "something secret and enormously powerful," has been dehumanized to the brute expression of an ivory Christ nailed to his bedroom wall with large spikes. (p. 8)

The spiritual dryness of Miss Lonelyhearts is echoed in his correspondents. Appealing to him as possessing the latent power of a Christ with the ability to redeem and educate them as to the right path for salvation, they are ignorant that he too is trapped by a similar spiritual dryness and ignorance of faith. "Sick-of-it-all" writes of the pain she must suffer from childbirth because her Catholic husband and religion say "no woman can be a good Catholic and not have children irregardless of the pain." (p. 2) Then there is "Desperate" who blindly questions the reason why she was born physically deformed:

> What did I do to deserve such a terrible bad fate? Even if I did do some bad things I didnt do any before I was a year old and I was born this way. I asked Papa and he says he doesnt know, but that maybe I did something in the other world before I was born or that maybe I was being punished for his sins. I dont believe that because he is a very nice man. Ought I commit suicide? (pp. 2-3)

In these and other instances, Lonelyhearts' immediate response is to call upon Christ for relief—but the relief is short-lived and without conviction.

Betty "the Buddha" offers a different type of salvation. Hers, like Buddhism, lies not in any conviction of belief or faith but rather in a specified plan of behavior. In many ways her simplicity of thought and action reflects the Buddhistic path of self-denial for

116

harmonic existence. But her plan is restricted to those who have the strength of will to follow it. Its limitation lies in its selectivity rather than in any inherent failure. Betty may be content, despite the surrounding world of chaos and disillusionment that sickens Miss Lonelyhearts. But her tranquility leaves Miss Lonelyhearts cold; "only violence could make him supple."

> Her world was not the world and could never include the readers of his column. Her sureness was based on the power to limit experience arbitrarily. Moreover, his confusion was significant, while her order was not. (p. 11)

Lonelyhearts, like his readers, needs a higher level of guidance—a moral rather than an ethical code of behavior. He argues against her reasoning and her answers for all the problems he confronts:

> As soon as any one acts viciously, you say he's sick. Wife-torturers, rapers of small children, according to you they're all sick. No morality, only medicine. Well, I'm not sick. I don't need any of your damned aspirin. I've got a Christ complex. Humanity . . . I'm a humanity lover. (pp. 12-13)

In short, religion is a failure in the New York of Miss Lonelyhearts because it has become as mechanized as every other aspect of city life. The entire suffering-supplication motif in the novel is standardized and simplified into an almost ritualistic pattern that loses all significance, all poignancy. The letters Miss Lonelyhearts receives degenerate from pathos to the level of a common joke, "all of them alike, stamped from the dough of suffering with a heart-shaped cookie knife." (p. 1) The City's pawnshops display the standardized paraphernalia of suffering: "A tortured high light twisted in the blade of a gilt knife, a battered horn grunted with pain." (p. 30) Miss Lonelyhearts sports aphorisms and trite cliches: "Life is worth while, for it is full of dreams and peace, gentleness and ecstasy, and faith that burns like a clear white flame, on a grim dark altar." (p. 1) But such statements have no impact in the modern City, for the Depression has left the inhabitants powerless and cruel. After reading "Desperate's" comically pathetic question as to why she must suffer throughout her life physically deformed, Miss Lonelyhearts' cigarette draws imperfectly and goes out. He takes it out of his mouth and stares at it furiously. His reaction is reflective of the Depression, filled with a self-centered and impotent fury.

Shrike mocks this rage in a letter to Miss Lonelyhearts:

> Dear Miss Lonelyhearts of Miss Lonelyhearts—
> I am twenty-six years old and in the newspaper game. Life for
> me is a desert empty of comfort. I cannot find pleasure in food,
> drink, or women—nor do the arts give me joy any longer. The Leop-
> ard of Discontent walks the streets of my city; the Lion of Discour-
> agement crouches outside the walls of my citadel. All is desolation
> and a vexation of the spirit. I feel like hell. How can I believe, how
> can I have faith in this day and age? Is it true that the greatest
> scientists believe again in you? (p. 35)

The answer, of course, is not forthcoming, but the question is naggingly repeated when Peter Doyle, Miss Lonelyhearts' counterpart
and assassin, appears in the novel. Crippled and stooped, with
the appearance of a "crushed insect," he is bored with his job and
his life and asks the age-old question of Miss Lonelyhearts: "What
is the whole stinking business for?" (p. 47)

> What I want to know is what in hell is the use day after day with a
> foot like mine when you have to go around pulling and scrambling
> for a lousy three squares with a toothache in it that comes from
> useing the foot so much. The doctor told me I ought to rest it for six
> months but who will pay me when I am resting it. But that aint
> what I mean either because you might tell me to change my job and
> where could I get another one I am lucky to have one at all. (pp. 46-
> 47)

Doyle's physical paralysis mirrors the spiritual-mental paralysis of
Miss Lonelyhearts as well as his questioning and helplessness.

The end result of all this paralysis is sadism. Man's agony, West
implies, when unveiled, turns vicious and resolves itself in either
an outward show of cruelty or inwardly directed masochism. West
first develops this motif in the novel by reducing the suffering of
the correspondents to such ludicrousness that the reader finds it
difficult not to laugh at rather than sympathize with their plight.
In short, the reader becomes as insensitive to the suffering presented as does Miss Lonelyhearts. The letters of woe become so
cliche-ridden in their outcries that their cumulative effect is negli-
gible on our feelings.

Cruelty appears during Miss Lonelyhearts' encounter with an
elderly man in a public toilet. An object of pity, homeless and
destitute, the Clean Old Man, as he is called in the novel, becomes

an object of ridicule and is sadistically tormented by Miss Lonely-hearts and his friend, Ned Gates:

> Miss Lonelyhearts felt as he had felt years before, when he had accidentally stepped on a small frog. Its spilled guts had filled him with pity, but when its suffering had become real to his senses, his pity had turned to rage and he had beaten it frantically until it was dead. (p. 17)

When Lonelyhearts physically assaults the Old Man, the attack is symbolically directed at all those who appeal to him for help:

> He was twisting the arm of all the sick and miserable, broken and betrayed, inarticulate and impotent. He was twisting the arm of Desperate, Broken-hearted, Sick-of-it-all, Disillusioned-with-tubercular-husband. (p. 18)

The cruelty marks the ultimate perversion of Miss Lonelyhearts' original instinct to help others. Like his youthful attempt at recreating a glorified sacrifice of an animal that turned instead into a bloody carnage, compassion in West's 1930's New York has evolved into a mockery of mankind's finer instincts and virtues. Our novel, therefore, becomes more than a tale of economic despair and unemployment in Depression New York. It is also an indictment of man's false belief in himself. For West, the Depression is found not primarily on the streets of the City, but rather within the human heart.

Chapter Four

[1]Bayrd Still, *Mirror for Gotham: New York As Seen By Contemporaries from Dutch Days to the Present* (New York: New York University Press, 1956), p. 300.
[2]Still, p. 318.
[3]Stephen Longstreet, *City on Two Rivers* (New York: Hawthorn Books, 1975), p. 235.
[4]*Ibid.*

[5]Federal Writers Project, *New York Panorama* (New York: Random House, 1938), p. 424.

[6]Still, p. 310.

[7]*Ibid.*

[8]Federal Writers Project, p. 203.

[9]Still, p. 318-9.

[10]*Ibid.*

[11]p. 309.

[12]*Ibid.*

[13]p. 308.

[14]p. 323.

[15]Federal Writers Project, p. 152.

[16]Still, p. 309.

[17]*Ibid.*, p. 335.

[18]pp. 314.

[19]*Ibid.*

[20]p. 312.

[21]p. 307.

[22]p. 301.

[23]p. 309.

[24]Elizabeth Nowell, *Thomas Wolfe: A Biography* (Garden City, N.Y.: Doubleday, 1960), p. 187.

[25]*Ibid.*, pp. 243-44.

[26]*Ibid.*

[27]Richard S. Kennedy, *The Window of Memory: The Literary Career of Thomas Wolfe* (Chapel Hill: University of North Carolina Press, 1962), p. 262.

[28]*Ibid.*, p. 263.

[29]Richard Kennedy and Paschal Reeves, eds., *The Notebooks of Thomas Wolfe* (Chapel Hill: University of North Carolina Press, 1970), II, 568.

[30]Paschal Reeves, ed., *Thomas Wolfe: The Critical Reception* (New York: David Lewis, 1974), p. 62.

[31]Thomas Wolfe, *Of Time and the River* (1935; rpt. New York: Charles Scribner's Sons, 1971), II, 420; henceforth all future references to this volume will be followed with the page number(s).

[32]James Light, *Nathanael West: An Interpretive Study* (Evanston: Northwestern University Press, 1971), p. 81.

[33]*Ibid.* p. 104.

[34]p. 109.

[35]Nathanael West, *Miss Lonelyhearts and the Day of the Locust* (1933; rpt. New York: New Directions Publishing Corporation, 1962), p. 22; henceforth all future references to this book will be followed with the page number(s).

CHAPTER V

The Post War Years: Saul Bellow's *Mr. Sammler's Planet* and John Cheever's *Bullet Park*

During the early forties, New York City remained largely an "American" city—American in that outside its obvious cultural superiority there was little to distinguish it from a typical, large midwestern city of the time. Its foreign-born population had assimilated well within its borders, and except for the small ethnic pockets of diversity, the population, as a whole, remained largely ignorant of this diversity of customs and traditions. The post-War years, however, saw significant changes in the *status quo* as many homeless and dispossessed people from Europe, South America, and Asia immigrated to the City which, for them, offered prosperity and hope. Unfortunately, such dreams were rarely realized. Post-War inflation created a shortage of jobs and housing, and due to the sudden influx of newcomers, the City's existing social and health-related facilities were greatly overtaxed. Slums grew at an alarming rate; the crime statistics increased; and for many, the City lost its charm as an appealing place in which to live.

Many, and especially the middle class, fled to a new land called suburbia—the semi-rural borders of the City. Here, along well-zoned, tree-lined streets, they created model communities where their children could mature in a safe and healthy atmosphere. No amount of money was withheld from the development of large modern schools, libraries, municipal pools, and recreation parks. But despite its auspicious beginning, suburbia too would eventually suffer from unprecedented growth, especially during the 1950's. Consequently, many of the problems associated with the City, such as inadequate housing, poor transportation, and pollution, followed the middle-class exodus to the suburbs. The problems were not as pronounced as those found in the City, but they existed nevertheless. As such, suburbia became not only the standard of post-War American culture, but also an extension of the City, destined to reflect both the City's desires as well as its failures.

In the meantime, the City remained as it has always remained—a melting-pot. By the early fifties, the major distinct ethnic groups—the Irish, the Germans, and the Italians—were assimilated New Yorkers. But the newcomers of the 1950's, the Puerto Ricans, were not so easily absorbed. Their customs and language precluded an easy transition into American society, where an ever-influential media frequently frowned on what appeared to be their failure to become "one" with the City. To assume that they could become Americans, and specifically New Yorkers, during the brief span of a decade was too unrealistic. Other ethnic groups had required many decades to effect the transition. Consequently, friction developed, and when the Puerto Rican community made demands on the existing infrastructure, the general populace saw not a people gradually merging into the mainstream of city life, but rather a vociferous and potentially violent foreign element.

For the established middle class of New York City, the Puerto Rican migration presented a tangible threat. Close to 800,000 White, middle-class New Yorkers fled to the suburbs during these years. All the white residents of an apartment on the lower East Side moved out after Puerto Rican threats were made against the landlord. The fear of violence in or near the Hispanic communities along the upper West Side of Manhattan resulted in many people refusing to leave their apartments after dark, and the formation of quasi-vigilante groups.

Further compounding this white, middle-class fear was the ever-increasing migration of Blacks from the South into the metropolitan area. The City's black population rose from 150,000 in 1920 to almost 750,000 by 1950 and continued to rise steadily during the next two decades. Concomitant with the Black migration was the ever-increasing impact of the Civil Rights Movement during the 1960's. The Black community of Harlem, which had remained relatively peaceful for almost half a century, now exploded in race riots and violent protests over alleged cases of police brutality and an "unresponsive" city administration.

Two incidents involving the Black community in 1964 epitomized the current trend of events. At the opening of the World's Fair in Flushing Meadow on April 22, civil rights agitators created a disturbance and hindered access to the Fair by jerking the emergency cords on subway trains servicing the area. The police were called in, and after some scuffling and a few bruised heads, the agitators were removed, denouncing the "discrimination practiced by the power structure of the City."[1] A far more serious riot, however, occurred a few months later on July 16. In an altercation between some youths in Harlem and an off-duty police officer, a youth with a knife was shot. The police report claimed that the officer had ordered the youth to drop the knife, fired a warning shot, and only when actually slashed by the youth fired twice more, killing the teenager. The Black community flared up in rage, condemning what they considered a totally unprovoked and unwarranted action on the part of the officer against a teenager "much smaller than himself."[2] Two days later, on the hot and humid night of July 18th, a full-scale riot broke out. Egged on by irresponsible community leaders, a mob attacked the 123rd Street police station and demanded that the officer be arrested for murder. Screaming "Killer cops!," the enraged mob clashed with police, ravaged through the heart of Harlem, fighting firemen, assaulting white people, menacing reporters, and looting stores. When peace was restored on July 23rd, the casualties totalled one person killed, 140 injured, and over 520 arrested. President Johnson ordered an FBI investigation and declared "American citizens have a right to protection of life and limb—whether driving along a highway in Georgia, a road in Mississippi, or a street in New York City."[3]

For many, the rioting was symptomatic of a malaise sweeping the City. Social commentators drew connections between the violence and the despair and frustration of living in New York. Crime statistics had steadily grown since World War II, and everyone, including the poor, felt its presence on the subways, on the streets, and in their apartment buildings. The gulf between the rich and the poor widened with the ever-increasing cases of welfare. Semi-skilled jobs had followed the middle-class to suburbia. Schools became overcrowded and declined in quality. Street congestion and air pollution increased as more and more people who worked in the City commuted by car. Increasingly, New York became a Gordian knot of modern urban problems. The job of governing it, according to the urban expert Robert Moses, was preposterous and impossible. To Jean-Paul Sartre, the City exhibited a cosmopolitan barbarism: "All the hostility, all the cruelty of the world," he noted, "are present in the most prodigious monument man has ever raised to himself."[4]

For the returning GIs of World War II, the City did not present the alluring facade that had captivated previous generations. The average GI saw his grim and brutal experiences overseas as a trial of will from which the lucky and successful would return to build a brighter future. Such a future could not exist on the hot and grimy streets of Brooklyn or the Bronx. The future lay in suburbia. Only here could a man and his family relax in peace, far from the hassles of city living. Only here could one build a home and not be obligated to a landlord's whim. And only here was an environment fit for the healthy development of children. Suburbia for the returning GI was not merely an alternative lifestyle—it was paradise.

A further demand for suburbia came from the thousands who had remained on the home front during the War years, employed in the various defense industries. Wartime rationing had slowed wartime spending, and many well-paid defense workers had set aside sizeable sums of money by 1945. They eagerly awaited the previously unavailable appliances and automobiles of post-War manufacturers. These people, along with the returning GIs, expected a better life. The War years, despite the hardships and rationing, had been financially prosperous when compared to the Great Depression, and post-War prosperity demanded a more high-keyed lifestyle. Suburbia was the answer.

One major example of this answer was the growth of Levittown in Nassau County, Long Island. On May 7, 1947, a *Newsday* headline broadcast that 2,000 low-cost housing units would soon be built on an eastern end of the flat Hempstead Plains south of Hicksville, and by the end of the month, the Levitt office was swamped with over 6,500 applications, mostly from veterans. The first homes were simple Cape Cods with 720 square feet of floor space. They were constructed on a mass production basis by non-union contractors. Each house included a kitchen, two bedrooms, a bath, a livingroom, sufficient closets, and a sizeable unfinished attic. Costs were kept down by having subcontractors compete for specific jobs, such as laying the slab or supplying the appliances. Through careful, economical planning, the Levitt homes became models of maximum housing for a minimum amount of overhead, and sold for a modest $6,990. Within three years, the Levitt plan transformed more than 40,000 acres of former potato farms into a thriving community with six schools, five shopping centers, five swimming pools, and ample parks and playgrounds. The community set the pattern for post-war suburban growth: first, housing evolved from the singly crafted house to the modular home of real estate developments; second, the profitability and demand for such housing resulted in a building boom in all areas adjacent to the City. In Nassau County alone the population doubled from 672,165 to 1,300,171 during the fifties.

Such rapid expansion, however, was not without problems. Much of the growth was haphazard and poorly zoned. Factories often rubbed shoulders with residential districts. Roads became congested and traffic unbearable. Since everyone drove cars, mass transit was ignored and would remain largely limited and ineffectual throughout the decade. Instead, new roads were projected and built at great expense, but were ironically referred to as either under construction or obsolete, but never completed. One classic example, the Long Island Expressway, was conceived in 1953 as a six-lane super-highway serving central Long Island. Intended to handle a peak load of 80,000 cars a day by 1970, it far exceeded this load by 1966 and on some weekends groaned under the weight of 170,000 cars. The world's "super" highway was soon dubbed the world's longest parking lot.

Besides traffic, suburbia began to feel unrestrained growth in other ways. One major problem was recreation. Suburbia had been envisioned as an escape from the burdens and unpleasantness of congested city life, and it put much emphasis on its ability to offer residents fine recreational living. But all too often parks and beaches suffered from chronic overcongestion and pollution. Lakes, rivers, and beaches lost their original purity as hords of suburbanite vacationers converged on them and frequently left behind garbage. Beaches also suffered from uncontrolled sewage disposal as communities poured billions of gallons of untreated waste into rivers and ocean fronts. One park supervisor warned the board of commissioners that the "general coliform count" was so high that it constituted exclusively "human excretion, human discharge, and you see it floating out here in the water."[5] The suburbanite suddenly found himself confronting the very problems he so desperately sought to escape in the City.

Thus, the suburban experience became a mixed blessing, offering a flawed Utopia, a garden of Eden, with problems. Some preferred to remain in the City. For them, suburbia offered no rewards that could compensate for the loss of New York's cultural excitement. Furthermore, a number of social critics feared that an insidious "group think" doomed suburbia to becoming a cultural desert of conformity. William H. Whyte noted that group participation and togetherness permeated a mindlessness where families "learn how to look happy."[6] Of course, no one then or now can be certain where suburbia is going. The suburban housewife has been largely replaced by the working woman of today. Divorce within the baby boom generation has precipitated a new type of single parent family, and for many the modern suburbia possesses nothing of the simplicity or blandness of the 1950s and 1960s. Tranquility has given way to turbulence. Suburbia is now a part of the extended City.

In Saul Bellow's 1970 novel, *Mr. Sammler's Planet*, the City is framed within modern dimensions. The physical presence of New York, as in earlier novels, is placed before us in all its beauty and ugliness with majestic buildings overshadowing squalid slums and Nature attempting to push through the filth and decay in the parks. But in Bellow's novel, this physical presence is merely a mask, a facade covering the City's spiritual significance and its impact on Artur Sammler, an aged Polish-Jew, attempting to come to grips with violence, disorder, and disillusionment. For him New York is the symbolic city of the world, a reflection of the past and an unnerving herald of the future—a combat zone where the memories of World War II are replayed in the subways and on the streets. It is a city of suicidal hedonism and the testing-ground for Western civilization.

For Sammler, memory is oppressive. A survivor of the Holocaust and a mass execution where he lost his wife but miraculously survived, he finds the contemporary City another battleground where a marginal civilization is fast dissolving. In an encounter with an elegantly dressed black pickpocket on a Broadway bus, he experiences the same element of fear, the same need for "lying low," that pursued him during the War years. These are the emotions of one who has survived the atrocities of war. They are conditioned reflexes, and essential for the modern urbanite.

Throughout the novel, the pickpocket, a symbol of violence, hovers on the fringes of Sammler's consciousness, a threatening yet strangely noble person, confident and in command of his equally violent environment and the opposite of the intellectual and ineffectual Sammler, who sees in the pickpocket "a mad spirit. But mad with an idea of *noblesse*."[7] Still, Sammler is a survivor, whereas the pickpocket's violence is ultimately self-destructive. Ironically, it is Sammler's ex-son-in-law, Eisen, who delivers the fatal blow. Eisen's world, too, is one of perpetual violence. He represents vitality without intellect, force without reason, the very state of war itself. In his attempt to break up a fight between the pickpocket and Feffer, a friend of Sammler's, he almost bludgeons the pickpocket to death. A horrified Sammler protests, but these protests fall on deaf ears, for Eisen sees the world as a violent landscape. He "educates" Sammler: "You can't hit a man like this just once. When you hit him you must really hit him. Otherwise he'll kill you. You know. We both fought in the war." (pp. 291-292) But the War is something Sammler is trying to forget. A victim of memory, the episode recalls to his mind his having been blinded in one eye by a crushing blow from a German's rifle butt thirty years ago.

Sammler's dilemma makes the City particularly brutal in his perspective. The daffodils and tulips struggling for a foothold in the park become combatants, polluted by the fallout of soot on their open and glowing blossoms. The sycamores with their "blemished bark" are "getting ready to cough up leaves," and the grass is all but "put out, burned by animal excrements." (p. 105) Water, a symbol of regeneration and life, becomes tainted with decay. Lilacs and sewage compose the warm spring current that runs along 15th Street. The Hudson River is unclean and especially insidious in the evening when amidst the bushes and trees along its shore lurks the danger of "sexual violence, knifepoint robberies, sluggings, and murders." (p. 181) Spring loses the "touch of winter" as it merges into the "summer rankness." The vest-pocket parks along upper Broadway offer no peaceful sanctuary. "The old-time poetry of parks was banned. Obsolete thickness of shade leading to private meditation. Truth was now slummier and called for litter in the setting—leafy reverie? A thing of the past." (p. 279)

The city-dweller's senses are equally assaulted. The requisites for survival are great. One has to,

> run, sprint, waft, fly over shimmering waters, you had to be able to
> see what was dropping out of human life and what was staying in.

127

> You could not be an old-fashioned sitting sage. You must train your-self. You had to be strong enough not to be terrified by local effects of metamorphosis, to live with disintegration, with crazy streets, filthy nightmares, monstrosities come to life, addicts, drunkards, and perverts celebrating their despair openly in midtown. You had to be able to bear the tangles of the soul, the sight of cruel dissolu-tion. You had to be patient with the stupidities of power, with the fraudulence of business. (p. 74)

Such demands are obviously too great for most. But Sammler is a survivor of even greater atrocities. He possesses a vitality that is at odds with his circumstances and surroundings. He cannot help his "style of striding blind," crossing busy intersections, lifting his rolled umbrella and pointing his intended route to the cars, buses, and speeding trucks bearing down on him from all angles. (p. 6) In short, he does not act like an old person. He does not "appreci-ate his situation, unprotected here by position, by privileges of remoteness made possible by an income of fifty thousand dollars in New York—club membership, taxis, doormen, guarded ap-proaches." (p. 5) In the parlance of the modern age, he does not take care of himself.

The City's youth orientation is especially perplexing and dis-turbing for him. Rather than reflect a positive, constructive devel-opment upon the past, the ideals of youth have degenerated into a brutal desire to offend, to dominate, and to shock. Thus, as a guest lecturer on H.G. Wells at a local college, he is confronted by an angry student, "a figure of compact distortion," who rises out of the audience, "extending violent arms and raising his palms like a Greek dancer," cursing and ridiculing his views as intellectually impotent: "Why do you listen to this effete old shit? What has he got to tell you? His balls are dry. He's dead. He can't come." (p. 42) Later, pondering this attack, Sammler is offended by the student's violent disregard of manners, the first sign of a declining civiliza-tion masquerading as,

> a passion to be *real*. But *real* was also brutal. And the acceptance of excrement as a standard? How extraordinary! Youth? Together with the idea of sexual potency? All this confused sex-excrement-militancy, explosiveness, abusiveness, tooth-showing, Barbary ape howling. Or like the spider monkeys in the trees, as Sammler once had read, defecating into their hands, and shrieking, pelting the explorers below. (p. 43)

On a more graphic level, Sammler is sexually "assaulted" by the black pickpocket who wishes to affirm his sexual potency and authority over Sammler. Forcing Sammler into an apartment lobby, the pickpocket exposes himself:

> The interval was long. The man's expression was not directly menacing but oddly, serenely masterful. The thing was shown with mystifying certitude. Lordliness. Then it was returned to the trousers. *Quod erat demonstrandum*, Sammler was released. The fly was closed, the coat buttoned, the marvelous streaming silk salmon necktie smoothed with a powerful hand on the powerful chest. The black eyes with a light of super candor moved softly, concluding the session, the lesson, the warning, the encounter, the transmission. (pp. 49-50)

Both encounters point to Sammler's overwhelming sense of powerlessness in an environment where sexual virility has become the sole determinant of one's ability to be right and superior. Wisdom and learning, the prerequisites of culture and civilization, have been abandoned for the primal laws of physical and sexual dominance. The rarified culture of New York City—its museums, libraries, and schools—is being replaced by the law of the jungle, the same laws that plagued Sammler during World War II. But during World War II he was younger; he could fight and apply his instincts for survival. As an old man in the modern city, in a new age, he wonders:

> It was a feeling of horror and grew in strength, grew and grew. What was it? How was it to be put? He was a man who had come back. He had rejoined life. He was near to others. But in some essential way he was also companionless. He was old. He lacked physical force. He knew what to do, but had no power to execute it. (p. 289)

He is also powerless in comprehending the sexual exploits of his promiscuous niece Angela. "Humankind," he feels, has "lost its old patience." (p. 162) The need for privacy is dead. Life now demands "accelerated exaltation, accepted no instant without pregnant meanings as in epic, tragedy, comedy, or films." (p. 162) He does not want to become foolish like many others his own age:

> It was amusing . . . old women wearing textured tights, in old sexual men, this quiver of vivacity with which they obeyed the sover-

129

eign youth-style. The powers are the powers—overlords, kings, gods. And of course no one knew when to quit. No one made sober decent terms with death. (p. 8)

Consequently, in Sammler's mind, New York City's preeminence as the symbolic City of the world is inherently warped. For him, it is a dubious distinction wrought from the City's extraordinary level of decay encompassing all times and all places. The City is a standard against which the collapse of Western civilization can be gauged. He finds the smashed telephone booths along Riverside Drive as indicative of an ancient barbarousness, "under the protection of civilized order, property rights, refined technological organization." (p. 7) From this standpoint, New York reflects an Asian or an African town:

> The opulent sections of the city were not immune. You opened a jeweled door into degradation, from hypercivilized Byzantine luxury straight into the state of nature, the barbarous world of color erupting from beneath. It might well be barbarous on either side of the jeweled door. (p. 7)

The derelicts and the drug addicts take on the appearance of Bombay or South American beggars, "beards clotted, breathing rich hair from their nostrils, heads coming through woolen ponchos, somewhat Peruvian." (p. 106) The prostitutes mirror the decadence of ancient Babylon, and the rush-hour subway is hauntingly similar to the mass execution graves of Nazi-dominated Poland. A friend's demonstration on the powers of a bullet reminds Sammler of the Zamosht Forest where he killed a straggling German soldier for clothes and food: "A second shot went through the head and shattered it. Bone burst. Matter flew out." (p. 139)

Riding on the Broadway bus, Sammler draws another connection between past and present. New Yorkers "mythologize themselves," he observes. (p. 147) Their clothes represent all the nations and times and places of the world. They reproduce the barbarian and the dandy, the buffalo hunter and the guerilla, the Guevara or the new Thomas à Becket. There is a possible vitality behind all of this, he feels; the City allows its inhabitants freedom to use their imaginations and rise above the "ordinary forms of everyday life." (p. 147) But there is a price often paid for such creativity, he concludes. It is the price of madness. The City's achievement possesses the seeds of an "animal of genius." But its frantic pace is diseased: "New York makes one think about the collapse of civilization, about Sodom and Gomorrah, the end of the world." He confides to his niece Angela, "The end wouldn't come as surprise here." (p. 304)

The City's spiritual decay, however, is an indictment of all Western civilization in general, a civilization possessed by a shocking iconoclasm and hedonism. All of Sammler's associates and friends are dangerously irreverent. Times have changed since he was a young Polish intellectual in England, a member of the H.G. Wells group of questioners and reformers. Things were beginning to be torn off their prominent pedestals in those days and especially during the years following the horrors of World War I. The atrocities of trench warfare had made Western man a cynical creature, cautiously viewing all the modern technological advancements of the day. But, Sammler recalls, the essential spirit behind this rejection tended toward constructive goals. Mores were challenged, but new ideas took their places. Underneath it all lay an elemental humanism, optimistic in tone, founded on the belief that mankind and civilization, while astray, could be returned to the right track.

But what hope, what sense of humanism, can survive the terrible despair and carnage of World War II? Sammler looks at his fellow New Yorkers and sees a hollowness of soul. The ultimate decline of civilization is evident not in its rebellion but rather in its lack of concern; the world becomes a place where right and wrong lose distinction and everything exists in an amorphous moral blur, where idleness, silliness, shallowness, distemper, and lust become justified and former respectability is abandoned. His despair is intensified after his unsuccessful lecture at the college. At odds with his young audience, impervious to his ideals and immersed in the "sacrament of shit," he is never more aware of how spiritually poor the age has become, of how all individuality is destroyed by a perverted community of thought: "Accept and grant that happiness is to do what most other people do. Then you must incarnate what others incarnate. If prejudices, prejudice. If rage, then rage. If sex, then sex. But don't contradict your time. Just don't contradict it, that's all." (p. 73)

A tabloid mentality, an aggressive invasion of privacy at the expense of decency and masquerading as a "search for truth," characterizes the age and Sammler's friends. Sammler, too, is infected with a curiosity that forces him to repeatedly observe a pickpocket in action on an uptown bus. But his concern is scientifically objective and preoccupied with the consummate individuality of the thief. His friends are unable to appreciate this. One, Feffer, is determined to get a tabloid expose of the criminal: "I wouldn't actually tangle with him," he reassures Sammler. "I'd never do that. He wouldn't even suspect I was there. But cameras can be introduced anywhere. They even have photos of the child in the womb. Somehow they got a camera in. . . . He'd never know. I assure you. Wouldn't be aware. Pictures could be valuable. Catch a criminal, sell the story to *Look*." (p. 123) Feffer's plan is inherently pointless. There is nothing constructive in his fascination with the criminal. It possesses only an element of voyeurism for anything intimate and personal, and as such, should be immensely successful in the new age where even the womb is not free from the inquisitive.

In Sammler's own family, privacy is dead. His niece Angela persists, against his protestations and obvious sense of delicacy, in relating every intimate detail of her sexual affairs. Even her clothes reflect the new age. "Little, after all, was concealed by her low-cut dresses." (p. 71) Her reports assume, as the novel progresses, the general tone of a "personal" newspaper column that masquerades the intimacies of everyone's sex life as "psychological" insight.

Underneath all the inquisitiveness, all the show-and-tell, lies, deeply buried, fear and despair:

> Life, when it was like this, all question-and-answer from the top of intellect to the very bottom, was really a state of singular dirty misery. When it was all question-and-answer it had no charm. Life when it had no charm was entirely question-and-answer. The thing worked both ways. Also, the questions were bad. Also, the answers were horrible. This poverty of soul, its abstract state, you could see in faces on the street. (p. 280)

New York City is a hedonistic city; and it is this hedonism that lends to all searches for truth, to all attempts to gain an insight into one's own personality, an element of selfishness that cannot help but be destructive and self-defeating at the core. New York can never be for Sammler a city of hope. He cannot enter into the liberal beliefs of his age, and he wonders if Western culture can survive universal dissemination. The problem lies in the limitless demand that this culture in all its seemingly limitless supply creates. The tantalizing dreams of the advertising age are in reality nightmares: "A full bill of demand and complaint was therefore presented by each individual. Non-negotiable. Recognizing no scarcity of supply in any human department. Enlightenment? Marvelous! But out of hand, wasn't it?" (p. 34)

Angela and her lover, Wharton Horricker, are devoted to the new hedonistic cult of the self. They are presented only in physical terms. Their clothes, hairstyle, foods, and sexual appetites define them. In the new age one rejects an intellectual position in favor of a specific lifestyle and Madison Avenue hype. Indeed, Horricker is *all* Madison Avenue, "some sort of market-research expert and statistical wizard." (p. 68) Sammler is aghast. Must the new age appear as sterile originality and false individualism, "in these forms? In these poor forms? Dear God! With hair, with clothes, with drugs and cosmetics, with genitalia . . .?" (p. 229)

In the end, New York represents the paradoxical state of mankind. In the Orwellian world of the City where values are reversed, sins become virtues and madness is insight. When Sammler alerts the police of a crime, he is informed that nothing can be done until he registers his complaint on a "waiting list" of priorities—justice reduced to mathematical *uncertainty*. His son-in-law Eisen, a half-deranged artist, is bound to succeed, according to Sammler, in such an environment, for here "madness is higher knowledge. . . . Power and money of course do drive people crazy. So why shouldn't people also gain power and wealth through being crazy? They should go together." (p. 65) Wallace, his nephew, too is infected with the instability of the New York entrepreneur. An odd parody of Franklin's *Way to Wealth*, he represents a new frenetic business philosophy where one sets up a new "enterprise," in the words of Feffer, redescribing the phenomena, and creating a feeling of going somewhere. (p. 111)

For Sammler, man has no escape from this dementia. Utopian societies and colonies on the moon as proposed by Dr. Govinda Lal are irrelevant. Man's condition will remain the same wherever he lives. Within the City reside the populations of the earth. Here, indeed, is the testing-ground for all mankind. New York City is the city of the world. "Ravage all," Sammler contemplates, "and what does death get? Defile, and then flee to the bliss of oblivion. Or bolt to other worlds?" (p. 135) Certainly, he concludes, there is no salvation in escape because man cannot escape from himself. Man must find a personal peace and, as he concludes in the death of his nephew, Dr. Gruner, "meet the terms of his contract." (p. 313) This is the final lesson the City teaches us, but it is a lesson that

frequently comes too late for the modern man, the New Yorker—
the man of the world.

Unlike the turbulent and violent environment of Artur Sammler's New York, the suburban world of Eliot Nailles in John
Cheever's *Bullet Park* is an apparent haven of tranquility. The reason for this, of course, is due to its distance from the City. Indeed,
Cheever even presents us with a suburban law of tranquility
wherein peace increases concomitant to one's distance from New
York. Consequently, the chief characters in the novel are frequently
thrown into paradoxisms of ever-increasing confusion whenever
nearing or within the borders of the City.

The tranquility of *Bullet Park*, however, is not without its limitations. The novel begins with a visual presentation of harmony that
is deliberately two-dimensional: "Paint me a small railroad station," Cheever asks the reader, "then, ten minutes before dark."[8]
Not only is the station's visual tranquility, with its "lamps along
the platform burning with a nearly palpable plaintiveness," presented in the medium of a picture, but the scene itself is set in the
twilight shades of obscurity. Similarly, the subdivision of Powder
Hill is presented at "an improbable distance" with its lights twin-
kling, chimneys smoking, and a "pink plush toilet-seat cover" fly-
ing from a clothesline. (p. 5) The perception is further distorted in
that it is presented from the point of view of an adolescent who is
angry with the "harmony," "cant," and "lechery" of Powder Hill
and especially of its having "leached from life that strength, malo-
dorousness, color and zeal that give it meaning." (p. 15)

Parallel to the visual harmony is a superficial social harmony
based on wealth. This is the subjective observation of Mr. Hazzard, a real-estate agent. For him the well-to-do Wickwires represent an ideal of suburban living. Indeed, they are "social workers"
in his canon, "celebrants—using their charm and their brilliance to
make things go at a social level." (p. 6) They are people who understand that giving cocktail parties contributes as much to the
welfare of the community as do the schools and municipal services. Their neighbors, the Ridleys, are distinguished in bringing
into the "hallowed institution of holy matrimony a definitely commercial quality. . . ." (p. 98) For them, the raising of children is like
the "manufacture and merchandising of some useful product"
produced in competition. (p. 98) With both families the rules of

suburban etiquette are followed to the exclusion of all human spontaneity. They are as artificial as Marietta Hammer's laugh, "the kind of laughter one hears in women's clubs, at bridge parties and in those restaurants that feature rich desserts." (p. 52) Parties are given in Bullet Park for the benefit of engaging in strained gossip and occasional backbiting. They are a time for boasting about one's career or the success of one's children. They are also a time for flirtation, of harmless adulterous exchanges. And rarely does genuine conversation intrude to spoil the evening. The suburban world of Bullet Park precludes such intimacy and demands only the facade of harmony and friendship from its inhabitants: "No one would get drunk, no one would fight, no one would likely get screwed, nothing would be celebrated, commemorated or advanced." (p. 236)

Underneath this harmony lies an economic determinism that dictates who is acceptable and who is not, who is to be invited into select circles and who is to be excluded. An individual is not judged by his character but rather by the cost of his home. The Wickwires are upstanding citizens who, according to Hazzard, are proud owners of a large white house with an estimated resale price of $65,000. The key word is, of course, "resale," for it embodies the very transitory and impermanent nature of the entire community where nothing is cherished or lasting. Houses are not noted for their architecture or history; only their economic value is featured.

The same values apply to their inhabitants. One of Nailles's principal concerns is the *financial* dignity of his job as a merchandizer of Spang, a mouthwash manufactured by the Saffron Chemical Company. His moderately high salary keeps him in good standing with his neighbors. But his job possesses little dignity beyond this, and Nailles is restive. If questioned about his occupation, he admits only to his being a chemist. He does not realize it, but this is fine for Bullet Park. Only the financial aspect of one's employment is scrutinized. So Nailles's repeated self-justification as to the supposed merits of his job is merely a form of self-reinforcement, psychological wound-dressing. Not even his own family is as concerned as he is about the benefits derived from using Spang or the destructive effects of bad breath:

> Sexual compatibility was the keystone to any robust marriage and bad breath could lead to divorce, alimony and custody suits. Bad

breath could sap a man's self-esteem, posture and appearance. Suspecting himself to be a sufferer, the victim would mumble into his shirt, hoping to divert the fumes downward. Bad breath recognized no class. Nailles had read in the paper that bad breath came between Lord Russell and his love. Bad breath could come between the priest and his flock, Nailles had observed, when Father Ransome breathed on him as he reached for the chalice. In Nailles's mythology the nymphs complained among themselves about the bad breath of Priapus. Bad breath drove children away from home. The wise statesman in his councils was not heeded because his breath was noxious. Bad breath was a cause of war. (p. 102)

Beyond the obvious visual contrasts, therefore, there is little to differentiate the suburban world of Bullet Park from that of the City. The superficial social and economic values are similar and inviolate. When Nailles finds it increasingly difficult to commute to his job in Manhattan, his dilemma is reflective more of his psychological turmoil and conflicts within his family than due to any true difference between the two environments.

Part of his confusion stems from his being a believer in the harmony of Bullet Park, but not realizing that it is a harmony based on ignorance and the desire to insulate oneself from the rest of the world. The suburban mind is etherized and ridiculously naive. Unlike Sammler, who is stupified by the inherent brutality of city life and its play upon his memory, Nailles has retreated into the cliches of the real estate advertisers. He intelligently disputes with his increasingly perceptive but depressed son Tony the merits of suburban living, but remains confused:

I hate lying and I hate falsehoods and when you get a world that admits so many liars I suppose you've got something to be sad about. I don't, as a matter of fact, have as much freedom and independence as I'd like myself. What I wear, what I eat, my sex life and a lot of my thinking is pretty well regimented but there are times when I like being told what to do. I can't figure out what's right and wrong in every situation. (p. 65)

In fact, Nailles cannot figure out what is right or wrong in *any* situation. His confusion exists on all levels. He has an unbounded love for his family, but it is an affection that frequently becomes excessively possessive and overprotective. It has, as Cheever notes, the ambivalant quality of a "limitless discharge of a clear amber fluid that would surround them and leave them insulated but visible like the contents of an aspic." (p. 24)

Such love mirrors the insulated suburban environment from which it springs. It is not a love that allows for development and true understanding. Consequently, Nailles sees his beloved son sink deeper and deeper into depression while he himself is trapped between the self-destructive poles of confusion and a narcotic withdrawal from reality. He never understands or can even begin to understand the moral or ethical implications of his world. He views the growing senility and suffering of his mother with a Job-like perplexity: "She had been in all things a fair woman—kindly, decent and loving—and that she should be cruelly smitten and left so close to death challenged Nailles's belief in the fitness of things." (p. 26) Nor does the intended murder of his son by Hammer jog him out of his confused state, for at the end Tony returns to school, Nailles to his narcotic addiction, and all is as "wonderful, wonderful, wonderful, wonderful as it had been." (p. 243) Nailles, consequently, like Sammler, is a victim of a psychological paralysis—albeit from a different source—but nevertheless related to an environment that not only links the characters but closes the gap between the City and the suburbs. The same problems exist in Cheever's world; they have merely taken on a different coloring in their new setting.

This "suburban paralysis" affects all the characters in Bullet Park and is continually reinforced by its environment. One of the preeminent influences on the characters is the ever-present daily ritual—ritual that is so entrenched that little, if any, variation from it is prohibitive. The life and death of Harry Shinglehouse is one example. The character is the embodiment of bland suburban values that offer little comfort during times of crisis. His obituary notice in the evening paper sums up his eminently respectable suburban life—had a wife and three children, ran for town council on the Republican ticket, employed in advertising. But when his existence is threatened by unemployment, he commits suicide by throwing himself under an oncoming commuter train, itself a fitting symbol of suburbia.

Even more telling is the lack of effect his suicide has on his fellow commuters standing on the waiting platform. So immersed are they in their daily routine of reading their newspapers, they fail to notice his leap before the train. Nailles is the only one who becomes gradually aware that Shinglehouse is missing after the express train passes. The comedy begins when he mentions it to Hammer who is also deeply absorbed in his newspaper. All that is left of the body is a brown loafer lying on the cinders. But life goes on as usual. When the 7:56 arrives, all except Nailles and his friend Hammer board it without concern. The incident, of course, is contrary to the suburban rule of happiness, and has to be repeated to the baffled police three times before action is taken. Nailles and Hammer have jobs to get to and reject the police's advice to come to the stationhouse, suggesting instead that the railroad police should be contacted. Only for a brief moment are the two men galvanized into some sort of transitory action that departs from the daily routine. Within it there is no exhibited concern for the loss of the man, and ritual takes precedence in the end. Nailles's concern can only be short-lived in a suburban setting that ignores the bizarre, unusual, or painful situations of life, and he abandons his plan of calling on the widow that evening because he can "think of nothing to say." (p. 61)

The sterility of Nailles's suburban feelings is again evidenced when he finds himself at an emotional impasse with his increasingly withdrawn son. When Tony completely rejects the suburban world around him and withdraws into his room "feeling sad," Nailles is confused and angry but envious of his son's momentary freedom from the restrictions of everyday ritual. Preparing for a party, he finds himself imitating his son by refusing to get dressed. His suit on the bed claims a "rectitude and a uniformity that was repulsively unlike his nature." (p. 237) But this is his false self-opinion. In the end, he dresses for the party and even becomes frantic when he discovers he has misplaced his wallet:

> "Oh here it is," cried Nellie. It was the pure voice of an angel, freed from the mortal bonds of grossness and aspiration. "It was in the pantry under the minutes of your last meeting. You must have put it there when you made your drink." "Thank you darling, thank you," said Nailles to his deliverer. (p. 239)

Drugs and alcohol increasingly exert control over Nailles's behavior. Their importance increases along with the growing disorder and confusion in his life. As his son lapses deeper and deeper into depression, he finds the suburban environment ineffectual in controlling his anxiety. He becomes mentally paralyzed and is unable to commute to the City without becoming chronically fearful. His ability to function as a traditional representative of suburbia is collapsing.

His loss of control, however, has nothing to do with any intrinsic difference between the City and suburbia. It is important to remember that in Cheever's world there is no absolute difference between these two environments, only an imagined, mythical difference supported by suburban clichés. When the peace of Nailles's home is shattered, suburbia "fails" to act as a restorative because it can never be one. It is too much like the City. In short, he realizes that without the suburban reinforcements, weak as they may be, an alternative formula for inner peace is needed. For him, this is drugs.

His retreat to drugs is understandable, if not logical. It represents in a dramatic manner the suburban desire to be insulated from everything painful or unpleasant. Pain and suffering are synonymous with city living. For Nailles they coexist as a principality, "lying somewhere beyond the legitimate borders of Western Europe. The government would be feudal and the country mountainous but it would never lie on his itinerary and would be unknown to his travel agent." (p. 48) In such faraway places people suffer and die. But not here in Bullet Park.

Consequently, his suburban imagination cannot grasp the reality of suffering. Such things are simply not permissible in his world. When Tony grows increasingly withdrawn, Nailles finds himself "raging on the train platform on his way to work":

> Why, of all the young men in Bullet Park, should Tony have been singled out to suffer a mysterious and incurable disease? It was not a question that he asked himself but a question forced onto him pitilessly by the world as it appeared to him from the first thing in the morning until dark. Cheerful and thoughtless laughter on the station platform merely made Nailles wonder angrily and bitterly why the sons of his friends were free to walk and run in the light while his son lay imprisoned. (p. 49)

As his world is further shocked out of its suburban complacency, he resorts to narcotics in order to first sustain his dream vision and later to enable him to commute to his job in the City. In these and other instances, he follows the typical pattern of addiction, using any excuse in order to justify the habit that masks the overall pain in his life.

Nailles's withdrawal is not unique, only his method. His wife, Nellie, is able to withdraw with the aid of a stiff cocktail. His neighbor, Hammer, finds harmony in yellow rooms. Each character in the novel has his or her own unique retreat. And in suburbia this becomes an essential need since the very formation of suburbia is founded on the need to withdraw, the need to reject the unpleasant world of jarring experiences.

But retreating also signals defeat. It is inherently static, if not destructive. Its victims are so immured from the world of experience, they can never mature or understand life in all its variety. Nellie is confused after attending an avant-garde show in Greenwich Village where the performers disrobe. Surprised and shocked by the show's content, she attempts to play the part of a modern, liberal woman but nevertheless finds herself caught in a violent series of juxtapositions, concepts of propriety, and her own natural excitability. On the train home, she is bewildered and miserable and only able to become partially restored when she is within the safe confines of her home. It is here, as Cheever notes, that "falsehood, confinement, exclusion and a kind of blindness seemed to be her only means of comprehension." (p. 32)

Like his parents, Tony also retreats, but his withdrawal has the quality of a spiritual retreat in that he re-evaluates his presence in the physical world and seeks solace in the comforting philosophy of a swamee. While his parents withdraw into their suburban idyll, he rejects the suburban pleasures they cherish. He feels as if their home were made of cards and easily destroyed. The sacred cows of suburban existence, such as the excellent school system and the country clubs, fall under his critical eye: "He said that French was all grief and English was even worse because he read more than the teacher. Then he said that astronomy was just a gut course and that his teacher was senile." (p. 112) He is disillusioned by his father's pep talks on the "rules of the game," the necessity for restricting one's freedom to a certain extent in order to enjoy the pleasures of suburban living. And he remains unmoved by his father's material generosity.

It is a generosity that is founded on good intentions in that it is the only form of generosity that Nailles can understand. But it likewise represents a post-War suburban consciousness at odds with a younger generation of different values. Cheever's intention is not to side with one viewpoint or the other, but rather to present conflicting beliefs. The dilemma faced by Nailles is similar to Sammler's, but now it disrupts the tranquility of suburban uniformity.

The second part of *Bullet Park* chronologically details the life of the highly intelligent but insane Hammer. The symbolism of his name is immediately apparent, and critics have not been at a loss to point out Hammer as the destroyer of Nailles's tranquility. But the significance of Hammer's presence is too easily ignored in light of the obvious. Hammer is not merely Nailles's nemesis. He represents the essence of evil and its ironic association with madness and chance, the kind of evil a suburbanite expects to find in the City and from which he so desperately wishes to escape.

The irony of Hammer's evil is that it evolves from a desire for order and tranquility, the same order and tranquility so dear to Nailles and his family. For Hammer, order is reduced to objective criteria—specifically the lemon-yellow room he so ardently pursues throughout his section in the novel. The room transcends all other needs, including the love of other human beings, and it is only in such a room that he feels he can become an industrious and decent individual.

Hammer is obviously insane, but his insanity bears the very stamp of the suburban consciousness. He has merely reduced all the suburban trappings of tranquility—the community, the block, the house, the family car—into one central object, a yellow room. Thus, his insane desires represent Cheever's final comment on the suburban lifestyle, for it too is as insane and as irrational as Hammer's schemes. Hammer possesses all the irrationality of insanity that Sammler finds in the City, but now it is transformed and shaped in a suburban image. There is no difference between the two worlds at this point—only an illusion of dissimilarity. Violence and death are sugar-coated, so to speak, and when we discover that it is Hammer's intention to kill Tony, it cannot come as a surprise. Cheever hints of this collapse early in the novel. The title itself, *Bullet Park*, forewarns the reader that violence is lurking somewhere within Utopia.

Other parallels between suburbia and the City exist. The value shifts which so frequently confront and confuse Artur Sammler are again present in Bullet Park. Nailles's sense of propriety and decency falls within the strict guidelines of Sammler's. And, like Sammler, his ideals have become outdated and artificial in the moral stagnation of the contemporary age. Value shifts confront and confuse both characters, but Nailles represents those who fail under trial while Sammler is one who is ignored by a world that no longer cares. Nailles also approximates the humanistic values of Sammler when he recollects the simpler days of his youth and the beauty of Nature, wild and unspoiled by housing developments:

> Nailles remembered the roads of his young manhood. They followed the contours of the land. It was cool in the valleys, warm on the hilltops. One could measure distances with one's nose. There was the smell of eucalyptus, maples, sweet grass, manure from a cow barn and, as one got into the mountains, the smell of pine. There were landmarks—abandoned farms—a stone tower and a blue lake. In the windows of the houses one passed one saw a cat, an array of geraniums, the face of a child or an old man. He remembered it all as intimate, human and pleasant, compared to this anxious wasteland through which one raced the barbarians. (p. 227)

A further parallel between the suburbs and the City can be seen in the graphic contrast between the beautiful and the ugly that so frequently occurs. As in the City, where a few blocks can separate vast disparities of economic and social lifestyles, the suburban environment of Bullet Park is equally dichotomous. In the first chapter, when Hazzard drives Hammer back to the railroad station, the station's rundown and decayed appearance belies the pleasant and peaceful neighborhoods they have just visited:

> Suburban waiting rooms are not maintained and the place had been sacked. Broken windows let in the night wind. The clock face was smashed. The hands of the clock were gone. The architect, so many years ago, had designed the building with some sense of the erotic and romantic essence of travel, but all his inventions had been stripped or defaced and Hammer found himself in a warlike ruin. (pp. 13-14)

Another ugly contrast is evident in the evening paper Hammer reads while waiting for the train. An article describing the annual dinner of the Lithgow Club that featured a "parade of sweethearts—wives of the members—which was followed by a demonstration of the hula given by Mrs. Leonard A. Atkinson who was accompanied by her husband on the ukelele" is found alongside an item mentioning the death of Mr. Lewis Harwick, "burned to death last night when a can of charcoal igniter exploded and set fire to his clothing during a barbecue party in the garden of his home. . . ." (p. 14)

Similar contrasts obtrude into the secluded and tranquil world of Bullet Park when Nailles comes across the "collection of broken refrigerators, television sets, maimed and unidentifiable automobiles, and always a few mattresses, rent, stained, human and obscene" dumped in a vacant lot near his home on the western fringes of town. This trash, the decay of the City, has become a permanent fixture within the ideal world he has striven so hard to create:

> The town clerk had explained to him that the cost and inconvenience of legitimate dumping outweighed the scrap value of the rubbish. It was cheaper and easier to drive up to Bullet Park from the city and dump your waste than to have some professional haul it away. No violator had ever been caught and prosecuted. The problem for Nailles was merely emotional—Nellie would call the clerk and a truck would haul the stuff away in the morning—but his anger at seeing his land disfigured and his sadness and unease at the human allusions of this intimate and domestic rubbish disturbed him. (pp. 21-22)

Nailles's uneasiness is symptomatic of the entire suburban consciousness attempting to create a world free from the violence and decay of the City but never totally isolated from its influence. Nailles and his neighbors believe that they are among the chosen, the gifted, the economically secure, able to stake a claim here on earth that is reflective of the promised land. But their dreams contrast severely with the reality around them, and if none of them is able to find happiness, it lies not in their having failed as suburbanites, but more in their being human. For it is human weakness—lust, fear, anger, and hate—that makes life unbearable within the borders of the City, and it is this weakness that follows city-dwellers to the suburbs.

Nailles and his neighbors find reminders of the City constantly at their doorsteps because human nature has not changed with their ideal environment. As a result, they are perpetually at odds with their ideals. City people have vandalized the beauty of Bullet Park with their garbage, but Nailles is likewise a destroyer of Nature. The early morning silence is punctured by the aggressive sound of gunfire, and Nellie is awakened to discover her husband "in his underpants on their broad lawn, firing his shotgun at an immense snapping turtle."

> The sun had not risen but the sky was light and in this pure and subtle light the undressed man and the prehistoric turtle seemed engaged in some primordial and comical battle. Nailles raised his

gun and fired at the turtle. The turtle recoiled, collapsed and then slowly raised itself up like a sea tortoise and began to lumber towards her husband. She had never seen, outside a zoo, so big a reptile, but it was Nailles, not the reptile, who seemed out of place in the early light. It was the turtle's lawn, the turtle's sky, the turtle's creation, and Nailles seemed to have wandered mistakenly onto the scene. (pp. 119-120)

Fittingly, Nellie's initial thought upon hearing the gunfire is that the City has finally invaded suburbia: "There had been riots in the slums and she wondered for a moment if the militants had decided to march out of the ghetto and take the white houses of Chestnut Lane by force." (p. 119) But the irony lies in the fact that it is her husband who is firing the gun. This then is the suburban dilemma, but Nailles and his neighbors remain ignorant of it throughout the novel. Only Hammer is aware of the subtle undercurrents undermining their lives. But he departs from our story to a hospital for the criminally insane while his neighbors continue to live within their delusions and, as in Nailles's case, artificially induced euphoria.

Chapter Five

¹Edward Robb Ellis, *The Epic of New York City* (New York: Coward-McCann, Inc., 1966), p. 586.

²*Ibid.*, p. 587.

³p. 589.

⁴Alexander Klein, ed., *The Empire City: A Treasury of New York* (New York: Reinhart & Co., 1955), p. 455.

⁵Marilyn E. Weigold, *The American Mediterranean: An Environmental, Economic and Social History of Long Island Sound* (Port Washington, N.Y.: Kennikat Press, 1974), p. 171.

⁶Edward J. Smits, *Nassau Suburbia, U.S.A.* (Syosset, N.Y.: Friends of the Nassau County Museum, 1974), p. 208.

⁷Saul Bellow, *Mr. Sammler's Planet* (New York: Viking Press, 1970), p. 294; henceforth all future references to this book will be followed with the page number(s).

⁸John Cheever, *Bullet Park* (New York: Ballantine Books, 1969), p. 13; henceforth all future references to this book will be followed with the page number(s).

POST-SCRIPT

Despite her many detractors, New York's pre-eminence as the cultural, economic, and social center of America remains inviolate. Her position in the American novel of the future is assured by the vastness of her dimensions—psychological as well as real. But how future novelists will attempt to deal with her perplexing ambiguities remains to be seen. The calophony of foreign tongues, the sudden changes (both cultural and economic) of inner-city neighborhoods, the urbanization of suburbia, plus a wide variety of other conditions, will inevitably create a host of new problems for the future novelist.

However, one problem will remain—the problem of perception. The novelist will still find himself limited by his medium, the printed word, a medium that is visual yet required to convey the other physical sensations of the City. The future novelist, like the novelists of the last two centuries, will be faced with the difficulty of capturing the sounds of the City's streets (the roar of the buses along Fifth Avenue, the taxicab horns, the jackhammers of the construction crews), the odors of the various New York seasons (rain-drenched summer afternoons, crisp autumn mornings, snow-clad winter nights), and the physical presence of the City (the smoothness of Central Park's rolling hills and the angular concrete harshness of lower Manhattan).

Added to this is the dilemma that the novelist's perception is essentially his alone. He has no way of accurately gauging his viewpoint with that of his fellow New Yorkers, many of whom are from entirely different cultural backgrounds. This will probably constitute the single most difficult obstacle faced by the future novelist of the City, for it bears with it the stigma of racism, either real or imagined. In his quest for realism, he may create, instead, a hotbed of contention disputing his purpose. He may be labeled as biased toward one ethnic group and prejudiced against another.

He may be ridiculed as a political stooge for the existing power in government. Or he may be condemned as a subversive or an anarchist. Considering the possibility of having such ominous charges leveled against him, he may abandon the novel altogether, or, far worse, develop it along lines that will be objectional to no one.

But even if the future novelist is able to avoid these pitfalls, he is still faced with the goal of creating a work of fiction that will be as timeless, as immortal as the City itself. Unlike the City, his novel cannot derive its immortality by simply being. New York's immortality is generated by its very size, its physical dimensions, which defy the vicissitudes of time. But the novelist must rely solely on the universality of his work. It must present characters and events that apply to all men at all times regardless of where they may live. And towards this end the City still offers the ideal landscape, for within its borders live the combined races of the Earth, each with its own specific custom, tradition, and language, each anticipating the arrival of the future novelist who will give them expression and place them firmly within the ever-developing landscape of the City.

BIBLIOGRAPHY

Bellow, Saul. *Mr. Sammler's Planet*. New York: Viking Press, 1970.

Cady, Edwin. *Stephen Crane*. Boston: Twayne, 1980.

Cheever, John. *Bullet Park*. New York: Ballantine Books, 1969.

Cooper, James Fenimore. *Home As Found*. 1838; rpt. New York: G.P. Putnam's Sons, ND.

Cooper, James Fenimore, ed. *Correspondence of James Fenimore Cooper*. New Haven: Yale University Press, 1922.

Davis, Merrell R., ed. *The Letters of Herman Melville*. New Haven: Yale University Press, 1960.

Dos Passos, John. *Manhattan Transfer*. 1925; rpt. Boston: Houghton Mifflin Company, 1953.

Ellis, Edward Robb. *The Epic of New York City*. New York: Coward-McCann, Inc., 1966.

Federal Writers Project. *New York Panorama*. New York: Random House, 1938.

Hillway, Tyrus. *Herman Melville*. Boston: Twayne, 1979.

Inge, M. Thomas, ed. *Bartleby the Inscrutable*. Hamden, Conn.: Archon Books, 1979.

Katz, Joseph, ed. *The Portable Stephen Crane*. New York: Viking Press, 1969.

Kellogg, Grace. *The Two Lives of Edith Wharton*. New York: Appleton Century, 1965.

Kennedy, Richard S. *The Window of Memory: The Literary Career of Thomas Wolfe*. Chapel Hill: University of North Carolina Press, 1962.

_____, and Paschal Reeves, eds. *The Notebooks of Thomas Wolfe*. Chapel Hill: University of North Carolina Press, 1970.

Klein, Alexander, ed. *The Empire City: A Treasury of New York*. New York: Reinhart & Co., 1955.

Light, James. *Nathanael West: An Interpretive Study*. Evanston: Northwestern University Press, 1971.

Longstreet, Stephen. *City on Two Rivers*. New York: Hawthorn Books, 1975.

Ludington, Townsend. *John Dos Passos: A Twentieth-Century Odyssey*. New York: E.P. Dutton, 1980.

Morris, Lloyd. *Incredible New York*. New York: Random House, 1951.

Nevins, Allan, ed. *The Diary of Philip Hone 1828-1851*. New York: Dodd, Mead & Company, 1936.

Nowell, Elizabeth. *Thomas Wolfe: A Biography*. Garden City, New York: Doubleday, 1960.

Plomer, William, ed. *Four Short Novels by Herman Melville*. 1946; rpt. New York: Bantam Books, Inc., 1971.

Reeves, Paschal, ed. *Thomas Wolfe: The Critical Reception*. New York: David Lewis, 1974.

Ringe, Donald A. *James Fenimore Cooper*. New York: Twayne, 1962.

Smits, Edward J. *Nassau Suburbia U.S.A.*. Syosset, New York: Friends of the Nassau County Museum, 1974.

Stallman, R.W. *Stephen Crane: A Biography*. New York: George Bruziller, 1968.

Still, Bayrd. *Mirror for Gotham: New York As Seen By Contemporaries from Dutch Days to the Present*. New York: New York University Press, 1956.

Untermeyer, Louis, ed. *The Poetry and Prose of Walt Whitman*. New York: Simon and Schuster, 1949.

Wagner, Linda W. *Dos Passos: Artist As American*. Austin: University of Texas Press, 1979.

Waples, Dorothy. *The Whig Myth of James Fenimore Cooper*. 1938; rpt. New York: Archon Books, 1968.

Weigold, Marilyn E. *The American Mediterranean: An Environmental, Economic and Social History of Long Island Sound*. Port Washington, New York: Kennikat Press, 1974.

Weisberger, Bernard A. *Reaching for Empire*. New York: Time Inc., 1964.

West, Nathanael. *Miss Lonelyhearts and the Day of the Locust*. 1933; rpt. New York: New Directions Publishing Corporation, 1962.

Wharton, Edith. *The House of Mirth*. 1905; rpt. New York: New American Library, 1964.

Wolfe, Thomas. *Of Time and the River*. 1935; rpt. New York: Charles Scribner's Sons, 1971.

INDEX

151